Shashi Deshpande's Fiction

A Woman's Journey

Shashi Deshpande's Fiction

A Woman's Journey

Pallavi Thakur

prestigebooks
INTERNATIONAL PUBLISHING

Published by
Prestige Books International
New Delhi 110 060
Ph. 9818755529
email: prestigebooks@gmail.com
website: asiabookclub.com

Associate Office
Concord, NSW 2137
Australia

ISBN: 81-7851-091-X

Printed at Chaman Offset Press, New Delhi 110 002

Contents

Dedicated to
my father Late Dr. R. Sinhasan
and
my mother Mrs. Uma Sinhasan

Preface

A country's history is a saga of emancipation and subjugation of its natives. Indian history too delineates the development of the civilization and country's merciless exploitation by numerous invaders. The whole Indian history can be divided into three parts: ancient India, medieval India and contemporary India. If we take a journey through these periods, we find a decline in human values and human rights. Indian land passed on from one invader to another. Men struggled to cope up with the new systems imposed by the new rulers and women found them placed at the receiving end both in the family and the society. Indian women enjoyed their rights and freedom in ancient India. Medieval India witnessed a barbarous reign which pushed women to the dark recesses. Purdah system and with it many other evil practices thrived.

The 1930s was a volatile period in which major steps were taken to eradicate inhuman social practices meant for women. The British along with many Indian social reformers took some important steps to curb the problems. The Indian freedom movement found women participating with valour and vigour. With the emergence of free India women found them surrounded by new dilemmas and apprehensions as they oscillated between traditional and modern roles. Women learnt to develop their own perspectives towards life. This new perspective developed a revolution throughout the world called Feminism.

Many writers throughout the world and in India produced feminist literature which portrayed subjugated women in myriad roles. Indian women writers of 1950s and 1960s such as Kamala Markandaya, Ruth Prawer Jhabvala, Anita Desai, Shobha De, Nayantara Sahgal revealed the emotional undulations and psychological turmoil of women. However, these writers failed to give any solution to women's problems which could be applied universally.

Shashi Deshpande's literature comes as a respite to Indian women as she is the only writer who does not advocate brutal assassination of relationships to secure female rights. She talks of developing and nurturing healthy relationships where everyone gets equal freedom. Her novels trace a woman's journey from childhood to old age in which she perceives relationships as 'Binding Vine' which are nurtured by her through 'That Long Silence.' Roots of self-abnegation and shadows of archetypes play an important role in her social conditioning. The complexities of life and feminine roles baffle her but after contemplation she manages to find a solution in 'A Matter of Time.' Deshpande's literature suggests 'Small Remedies' which act as a panacea to women's traumas.

The present book traces feminism as a literary revolution in India. It voices Indian women's predicament in phallocentric society as witnessed by Shashi Deshpande.

This book would have not taken its present shape without the help and assistance of some people who have left an indelible mark on my life. I owe my extreme indebtedness to my parents for my existence and allowing me to understand and experiment with life. My father has been my constant source of inspiration. I owe him whatever I am today. I grew around my mother for whom femininity was never a weakness but strength. My brother taught me the meaning of family and relationships. My husband always encouraged me to realize my dreams. My supervisor, Dr. Rashmi Gaur, was more a mentor than a guide. This book is a message of gratitude to her. I would like to thank Dr. Gopal Ranjan, Director General, COER who taught me that diligence leads to success.

I would also like to thank almighty for bestowing me with two beautiful sons, Akshat and Keshav, who taught me that a pinch of excitement can add multiple positive flavours to life.

I am also grateful to the staff of various libraries particularly, SCILET, Madurai, for making available to me all the required material during the completion of this work.

Feminism: A Revolution to Empower Women

Feminism is a movement which advocates granting the same political, social, and economic rights to women as those enjoyed by men. Throughout the world, women have been deprived of their basic socio-legal rights by a patriarchal order. In the domain of patriarchal culture, woman is a social construct, a site on which masculine meanings get spoken and masculine desires enacted. The factor which changes a girl into a woman with a finality is not simply her anatomy, but the process of social conditioning which influences and moulds her psyche to desire and pursue traditionally accepted and encouraged feminine roles only. To change the conventional image of women constructed by the orthodox society, it is necessary to discourage the habit of defining woman as an essence whose nature is determined biologically and whose sole identity is to produce human species. Twentieth century has witnessed a growing awareness among women regarding their desires, sexuality, self-definition, existence and destiny. Bell Hooks writes in *Feminism is for Everybody: Passionate Politics*:

> Suddenly more and more women began to either call themselves "feminists" or use the rhetoric of gender discrimination to change their economic status. The institutionalisation of feminist studies created a body of jobs both in the world of the academy and in the world of publishing. (10)

Women's efforts to seek their independence and self-identity started a revolution all over the world which was termed by analysts and critics as 'Feminism.' In the early stages of the revolution, the feminists and suffragists were condemned by the patriarchal society for adulterating the minds of women with the idea of liberation from their suppressed state and encouraging them to eschew the blind subordination to the established traditional dogmas. However, soon it blossomed into a comprehensive ideology and provided a conceptual basis to women's struggle to overcome all types of exploitation and attain autonomous selfhood. The issues addressed by the feminist movement have also been actively advocated by the literary writers of different countries. Their expository and creative writings have significantly encouraged and shaped the feminists' struggle to empower women and help them transcend their deprived status. Successive writers have raised women's issues by expostulating and examining their subordinate situation in the cotemporary society. In their work, they have supported and propagated matters related with the suppressed state of women, which greatly contributed in bringing about a change in the social milieu. A discernible recent shift in feminist literature is from the representation of women's victimization to that of their resistance. Although the feminists and feminist writers have been successful in achieving the legal rights for women, yet much has to be done at the social level. Different countries having different religions and cultural mores have a new tale to recite about the plight of the modern women, their dilemmas and conflicts, and their efforts to achieve self-identity and independence. The contemporary writers are still striving to provide liberation to the female world from the debilitating socio-cultural constraints and oppressive myths of their respective countries. The journey from self-effacement to self-actualisation is yet to be covered.

The Architects of Feminist Writing in Europe and America

American and European societies have been traditionally dominated by the race of men. Till the beginning of the twentieth century, women lived in servile domesticity and were denied basic human rights. It was in 1920 that the women's right to vote was finally won by the feminists in the USA. Feminist writing and criticism began the day when women tried to express their deprived state in writing. It is difficult to trace the first feminist writer because many writings went unnoticed and unpublished.

But we can count Mary Wollstonecraft's *A Vindication of the Rights of Woman* (1792), Virginia Woolf's *A Room of One's Own* (1928), Simone de Beauvoir's *The Second Sex* (1949) and Betty Frieden's *Feminine Mystique* (1963) as revolutionary feminist texts, which brought about a fundamental change in the perspective of women towards their lives in Europe and America.

Mary Wollstonecraft's *A Vindication of the Rights of Woman* (1792) has been treated almost exclusively as a feminist manifesto, an unequivocal defence of women's rights. She raised her voice against sexual discrimination prevalent in the society and expounded that women should have equality of status. Sushila Singh writes in *Feminism: Theory, Criticism, Analysis* that Mary Wollstonecraft advocated granting of educational, legal and professional rights to women:

> Mary Wollstonecraft is the first crusader who articulated very powerfully the causes of women's subjugation and its perpetuation in the society. Rooted in the realities of her time, she virtually anticipated all the demands of the woman's movement—education, legal representation, the right of vote, the right to property, and admission to profession. (1997· 50)

In her discussions she has included many claims integral to modern feminism—coeducation, economic independence and legal equality—which express her concern for the inferior state of women in contemporary Europe. Her narration presents a grim picture of an oppressive reality. Women were not allowed to participate in public and political meetings. They were also denied the right of franchise. They were routinely provided with basic education, whereas higher education was strictly reserved for men. Mary Wollstonecraft's letter to M. Talleyrand-Periord, a French diplomat, which is illustrated in *A Vindication of the Rights of Woman*, shows her deepest concerns for women education. She requests him to respect the "rights of women" (4) whenever the amendments in the constitution are discussed. She writes:

> But, if women are to be excluded, without having a voice, from a participation of the natural rights of the mankind, prove first, to ward injustice and inconsistency, that they want reason—else this flaw in your NEW CONSTITUTION will ever shew that man must, in some shape, act like a tyrant, and tyranny, in whatever part of society it rears its brazen front, will ever undermine morality. (3)

Though Mary Wollstonecraft wrote about the deprived state of women in Europe, yet the book strangely had practical impact on contemporary mainstream literary criticism. Still, it is a definite precursor of revolt against the economic, intellectual and social restrictions on women and is a major statement of female potentiality.

Another feminist writer, Virginia Woolf, not only advocates intellectual emancipation of women, but also encourages them to fulfil their responsibilities as women. Her book *A Room of One's Own* elucidates her feminine principles. She feels that men and women are interrelated and therefore subjugation of one by the other destroys the harmony and happiness of life. She points out that patriarchy has deprived women of self-expression and self-improvement. The book enunciates that only when women are considered as human beings and are provided with education, they will be able to contribute to the overall development of the society. She believes that women possess potential, talent and strength with which they can dissolve their secondary status in the society, but their energy requires to be utilised in a proper direction. Virginia Woolf mentions in *A Room of One's Own* that "Shakespeare had a sister" who "died young" and thus "never wrote a word" (105). She believes:

> this poet who never wrote a word was buried at the cross roads still lives. She lives in you and in me, and in many other women [. . .], for they are washing up the dishes and putting the children to bed. But she lives; for great poets do not die; they are continuing presences; they need only the opportunity to walk among us in the flesh. (105-6)

Virginia Woolf has drawn some very remarkable and outstanding women characters in her novels. Rachel in *The Voyage Out* and Katherine in *Night and Day* want to go beyond the established social norms to achieve a sense of fulfilment. *To the Lighthouse* delineates her concept of a complete woman through the character of Mrs. Ramsay. Woolf's earlier women characters express suppressed state of women, whereas Mrs. Ramsay successfully carries out all her roles as a woman. Mrs. Ramsay symbolises the true feminism, which, in essence, is the uninhibited liberation of the self. Thus Virginia Woolf can be summarised as a successful feminist writer who has given a new image to women of her time.

Simone de Beauvoir's *The Second Sex* was published in 1949 and translated into English in 1953. The book reveals the true picture of subservient female, trained deeply to suit the masculine needs. She has exposed the patriarchal society which celebrates the ideal woman—devoted to domestic duties, religious, modest in dress, silent unless spoken to, and deferential to men. Beauvoir has talked about the subordination of women which they are subjected to at every stage of their lives, obliterating their individuality and restricting them to lead a passive life from childhood to motherhood. She has categorically analysed every stage of a woman's life and reveals to us with transparency the feminine world, its perspective towards life and its way of perceiving men and their world. She holds the society responsible for developing the feminine qualities in women and restricting their talents to a limited frame of family life. She writes in *The Second Sex*:

> Thus the passivity that is the essential characteristics of the 'feminine' women is a trait that develops in her from the earliest years. But it is wrong to assert that a biological datum is concerned; it is in fact a destiny imposed upon her by her teachers and by society. (19)

The Second Sex has to be accepted as a serious treatise on feministic ethos and issues which not only exposes the hidden facets of a woman's life, but also criticises the society for setting different codes of behaviour, action and manner for women. She has critically analysed the forbidden state of women and termed them as the second sex due to their secondary status in the society. Simone de Beauvoir appears to be realistic in her approach towards women's suppressed and subjugated life.

Betty Friedan is considered as a well-known feminist writer of America. She founded her own women's organisation called NOW (National Organisation of Women). By 1970s the movement of Feminism which was propagated by the middle-class American women established its roots in the whole of America. It was Betty Friedan's book *The Feminine Mystique* (1963), which created awareness among women about their deprived state in the post-war society. The book is a harsh statement of male superiority and female subjection. It criticizes the evident sexual discrimination against women which is condoned by the society and hence pushes women to recesses of domestic life. Nancy J. Hirshmann condemns society for constructing and dictating social behaviours in *The Subject of Liberty: Towards a Feminist Theory of Freedom*:

> This construction of social behaviours and rules comes to constitute not only what women are allowed to do, however, but also what they are allowed to be. (2003: 11)

She has elaborately discussed the problems of middle-class American women who become lethargic by leading a monotonous family life. The book exhibits the gradual change in the image of subservient American housewives and the open opposition it received from the patriarchal society. It traces the process of the American women's evolution from their dormant and passive state to the acknowledgement of their strength and power, simultaneously analysing the stifling norms associated with their femininity. It can be stated that Betty Friedan's book had a major role in initiating the feminist revolution in the United States of America. She comments in the epilogue of *The Feminine Mystique:*

> It is twenty years now since *The Feminine Mystique* was published. I am still awed by the revolution that book helped spark. It is a mystery to me that I was able to put it together, at the time it was needed, and that women, and men, even now stopped me on the street, and remember where they were when they read it—"in the maternity ward, with my third kid, and then I decided to go to the law school." (ix)

In America black women also gradually became aware of their suppression due to racial as well as sexual discrimination. Black women were maltreated and discarded by white as well as black men. They were doubly enslaved in white patriarchal, racist society. Slavery, which was once an inseparable part of the American society, never permitted black men to create a family as they had no strength, power or independence to provide security to it. Even those black men, who consciously or unconsciously made one, left their families to be looked after by their women. Thus the Afro-American women were vulnerable and open to racial, sexual and political exploitation. Patricia Hill Collins writes in *Black Feminist Thought: Knowledge, Consciousness and the Politics of Empowerment*:

> Taken together the supposedly seamless web of economy polity, and ideology function as a highly effective system of social control designed to keep African-American women in an assigned subordinate place. This larger system of oppression works to suppress the ideas of black women intellectuals and to protect elite white male interests and world views. (5)

Marian W. Stewart (1803-1879) is the first US Black woman who delivered lectures in public touching political issues. She articulated the social issues responsible for the negative images of Black women. According to her, race, gender and class operation were responsible for the subjugation of Black women. Her talks motivated many Black women and they became successor of her feminist ideology. Anna Julia Cooper is among the early feminists who discussed the plight of black women and their status in America. She advocated the granting of the right to higher education to them in her book *A Voice from the South* (1892). The black feminists were motivated by the revolutionary ideas of white feminists and subsequently many great black feminist writers like Toni Morrison, Alice Walker, and Gayl Jones communicated their black feminist impulse through their literature in 1970s. Bell Hooks explains:

> Very little serious literary scholarship had been done on works by black women writers prior to feminist movement. When Alice Walker acquired fame, she participated in the recovery of the work by writer Zora Neale Hurston, who shortly became the most canonized black women writer in American literature. (21)

Toni Morrison in her essay *What the Black Woman Thinks about Women's Lib* lays bare the difference in the status and treatment of black and white American women. She vociferously raises the issue of feminine emancipation in her literature. She is the first black woman to receive the Nobel Prize for Literature. In her novel *Sula* (1973) she talks about the lost identity of women in a chauvinistic society. Her female protagonist Sula is an enfant terrible who resists the established dogmas of the society related to women and strives hard to achieve self-identity. In her novel *Beloved*, which won for her the Pulitzer Prize in 1987, she describes the slavery system and the pathetic condition of black women within it. *Beloved* is a saga of grit and courage, the combination of the strength and constraints of a woman who is the mother, and happens to be a black slave in a society, which is bifurcated by dominant racial hatred into two sections—the ruler and the ruled, the master and the slave. Sethe, the female protagonist's decision to liberate her children from the evils of slavery leads her to attempt their murder. Thus Toni Morrison has touched the core issues of slavery and black suppression in her novels and has given a realistic picture of black women as victims.

Another major black feminist author, Alice Walker critically interrogates and deciphers the physical and sexual exploitation of black women by black men in her first novel *The Third Life of Grange Copeland* (1970). Another novel *Meridian* (1976) illustrates the refusal of its eponymous protagonist to accept the idealized image of black motherhood. She revolts against the racist and sexual oppression of black women and participates in civil rights demonstrations. She has realistically described the change desired by black women in their subjugated status.

Gayl Jones, another significant black feminist author, has evaluated the effect of stereotypes on the psychology of black women. Ursa Corregidora, the female protagonist of her novel *Corregidora* (1975), finds it difficult to free herself from the deified stereotypical image of ancestral women who meekly surrender to suppression and subjugation in their lives. It creates friction and disharmony in her relationship with her husband Mutt. Thus we can conclude that these writers advocated a feminist emancipation of black women by representing their pathetic state. They have communicated the traditional modes of oppression of black women in their own community and also by the dominating whites. Their language and imagery also successfully project the reality of black women's lives and are also an assertion of the validation of their feminine identity. Collins summarizes:

> According to many African-American writers no matter how oppressed an individual woman may be, the power to save the self lies within the self. Other Black women may assist a black woman in this journey toward personal empowerment, but the ultimate responsibility for self-definitions and self-valuations lies within the individual woman herself. An individual woman may use multiple strategies in her quest for the constructed knowledge of an independent voice. (119)

Thus we see that the conservative social norms and myths of feminine behaviour were challenged by women in Europe and America. The new climate recognised the vital contribution of women to the progress of humanity and sought a change in the social parameters. Women stepped forward to transcend the image of stereotypes in order to attain individuality. Although the acceptance and popularity of the feminist credo was initially propagated by socio-political factors, yet the important and vital role played by literature in popularising the idea of female emancipation, equality and empowerment can never be undermined. Mary Wollstonecraft, Simone de Beauvoir, Virginia Woolf and Betty Friedan created a general awareness among women about their marginalized status and the futility of their existence. Many other writers must have raised the issue of women emancipation earlier too, but their writings did not receive desired attention, appreciation and consideration. In the absence of any documentary proof, the above-mentioned writers can be accepted as architects of feminist literature. Gradually many successive writers came forward and advocated the concept of feminism through their work.

Feminism as a Literary Movement in India

Literary works present avant-garde constructs which often become the basis of revolutionary social transformations. They not only embrace in themselves the social, cultural or mythical backgrounds of their native land, but also expose the fragments of alienation present in different segments of human life and its predicament. Literature therefore has always been an effective vehicle of fundamental changes. To a large extent, the popularity of feminist ethics in India has also been generated by the 'new' image of women presented by literary writers in their works. Many critics have tried to trace the decline in the status of Indian women by rummaging its history. Geraldine Forber explains in *Women in Modern India:*

> Some reformers simply commented on wars and invasions, claiming that political disorder inevitably led to restrictions on women's education and mobility. A number of reformers located the decline during the time of Smritis, that is, to a period when the vast body of law codes such as the Manusmriti, commentaries, epics most prominently the *Mahabharata* and the *Ramayana*—and Puranas or stories of the Gods were written. These theorists argued that the decline in women's status could be traced to these writings. But most of the reformers blamed Muslim rule. (16)

The abolition of certain evil practices against women in the preceding centuries had also created a much-needed awareness in the society for imparting a better status to women. It was during the British rule in India that many relevant changes were made in order to ameliorate the pathetic condition of women. The Viceroy Lord William Bentik banned Sati in 1829. Social reformers like Raja Rammohun Roy had also supported this move. Similarly, remarriage of widows was sanctioned in 1856 and in 1929 a law was passed prohibiting child marriage. The most difficult task in India at that time was to educate women, because only a few women belonging to the families of zamindars were able to receive basic education. Many teachers, as well as social workers, considered it a necessity and started many educational institutions for women. In 1850s Ishwar Chandra Vidyasagar started many primary schools in the villages of Bengal. Arya Samaj, founded by Swami Dayanand, also propagated women's education. John Drinkwater Bethune established the first women's college in India in Calcutta in 1849. In 1851 Jotiba Phule came forward to educate the scheduled caste girls in Poona. Since then there has been no looking back, as women also started clamouring for education for which they had been indifferent for ages. These attempts provided the much-needed impetus and Indian woman took a hesitant step towards social emancipation. Many great Indian women writers appeared on the scene who represented the educated group of Indian women. Toru Dutt, Cornelia Sorabji, Shevantibai Nikambe, Krupabai Santhianathan and Smt. Swarnkumari Ghosal are some of the prominent women writers of this time. The literature produced by these women writers may not possess many literary merits, but it highlights the pathetic condition of women belonging to different sections of society. Geraldine Forber writes in *Women in Modern India* about the social reforms during British regime which led to the social emancipation of Indian women but simultaneously it overlooked their financial, psychological and physical needs:

> Because social change—in British terms "social reforms"—became such an important issue, our accounts of Indian women in

> the early part of the nineteenth century are often embedded in discussions of sati, child marriage, widowhood, polygamy and prohibition on education. These issues dominate the women's work and occupation values and emotional lives, and health and physical well-being. (11)

However the dilution of rigid social norms eventually propagated a liberated modern outlook among women. The change in the social milieu and its effect on the status and psychology of women encouraged the Indian writers to take cognizance of women's issues. Many outstanding regional writers—Homen Borgchain, Narayan Sanyal, Bimal Mitra, N. Mitra, Prem Chand, Yashpal, Nagar, Ashk, to quote a few—also wrote about this under-privileged class, critically reflecting the prevailing inhumane practices and atrocities in their work. Though the English prose writing in India was started by Raja Rammohun Roy, the novels of Bankim Chandra and Lal Behari Day are accepted as the first authentic examples of fictional writing in English. Mantagini, the female protagonist of Bankim Chandra's *Rajmohan's wife* (1864), is a woman who values her feelings and affirms her individuality. She represents those Indian women who protest against conventional mores and break the barriers of self-abnegation and denial. Lal Behari Day's *Govinda Samanta* is a realistic novel, which describes the socio-economic changes occurring in contemporary society. Women characters of the novel—Aduri, a widow who kowtows to evil practices related with women and Malati, a rebellious woman who is not ready to succumb to the atrocities of her mother-in-law—form only a part of the plot which adroitly demonstrates the leap from traditional to modern womanhood. The next generation of writers which appeared just before the Second World War, i.e., in the 1930s, picked up existing social customs and constraints as themes of their work. The first major thrust in Indian English writing came in the mid-1930s when the big trio—R.K. Narayan, Mulk Raj Anand and Raja Rao—appeared on the scene. Their work created awareness about the emerging Indian English literature. R.K. Narayan and Bhabani Bhattacharya portrayed modern women protagonists like Rosie in *Guide* and Kajoli in *So Many Hungers* respectively. Mulk Raj Anand and Raja Rao also delineated sensitive women characters in their novels. R.K. Narayan has depicted two kinds of women characters—one group possesses a traditional mind-set, while the other seeks freedom from constricting social norms. The conventional group contains women who are devoted mothers, aunts, grandmothers and wives—like the wives of Margayya (*The Financial Expert*), Srinivas and Sampath (*Mr. Sampath*) and Natraj (*The Man-Eater of Malgudi*). Though R.K. Narayan has portrayed some strong women protagonists, yet in most of his novels women are not treated with equality. In comparison to him, Bhabani Bhattacharya's novels possess round women characters who are integral to the development of the plot. His women characters, though somewhat dominated by their male counterparts and patriarchal customs, are still full of life and hope to have a better future. Kajoli in *So Many Hungers*, Meera in *A Goddess Named Gold*, Sumita in *Shadow from Ladakh* are optimistic women. To Bhattacharya, women are a source of strength and thus their contribution is significant not only to their families, but also to their country. Raja Rao and Mulk Raj Anand have not taken up the theme of women's emancipation independently. Their novels concentrate on the socio-economic issues of their times, exposing the harsh facts and realities of life. Feminist issues are only a part of their overriding concerns. However Anand's protagonist Gauri in *The Old Man and the Cow* is a fine example of his idea of emancipated woman.

With the attainment of independence, various reforms were made by the government to ensure development in the country. Soon, a new sphere of literature appeared where the writers wrote on themes projecting the miseries and complexities of human lives and concentrating on individual predicament. The mid-1950s and 1960s mark the second important stage of Indian English writing, when writers like Arun Joshi, Anita Desai, Kamala Markandaya, Ruth Prawer Jhabvala, Shobha De and Nayantara Sahgal came out with their works that changed the face of Indian English novel. They have opened up a new vista of human nature and man-woman relationship. The problems discussed in their novels are individual, rather than universal. These writers have projected the inner psychological turmoil of human beings surviving in different sections of the society.

Anita Desai has portrayed the tyrannies, torture and violence faced by women in Indian society. She has stressed the disturbed psyche of women which makes them appear neurotic. Shattered by their stifling atmosphere, her women characters become depressed and helplessly suffer. Most of her women characters lack the spirit of viewing life with optimism and fail to overcome their existing traumas and apprehensions. Maya in *Cry, the Peacock* is unable to understand her husband who has a practical approach towards life. Raka in *Fire on the Mountain* is a product of a broken marriage who has witnessed the violent attitude of her father towards her mother. The brutality of her father destroys the humanity in Raka. She sets the mountain on fire and rejoices in her act. Sita in *Where Shall We Go This Summer?* lives a life of comfort and ease with her husband, who is flexible and understanding. At the time of her fifth pregnancy she develops a psychological imbalance during the gestation period. To escape the reality of her life, she takes refuge at the island of Manori with the thought of getting blessings of his dead father who was known for performing miracles among the local people. It not only disturbs the smooth course of her marital life, but also pushes her children to the darkness of the island. Monisha in *Voices in the City* commits suicide as she finds no way out of the monotony of her life. Anita Desai has also projected the pathetic condition of Indian widows through her character Mira Mashi in the novel *Clear Light of the Day*. She is one of those contemporary writers whose themes revolve around the female world. Her women characters though lack strength, vitality, valour and hope, and are normally unable to develop a positive approach towards life. Her women characters are feeble and engrossed in their pain, which inculcates in them a devious state of mind restricting them from initiating relevant and authentic changes in their lives. Most of them lack the power to analyse their pathetic condition and cannot overcome their neurotic state. Her novels mostly exhibit the disturbed psychology of bereaved women and their lassitude due to the stifling atmosphere in which they have to survive. Her fiction does not talk about the emancipation of women either intellectually or morally. Her themes are not universal; rather they talk about individual women and their emotional and psychological turmoil.

Ruth Prawer Jhabvala is another contemporary Indian English novelist who has portrayed strong women characters in her novels: Her novels project the post-Independence Indian society which consisted of Indians as well as Britishers. They portray beautiful and vivid pictures of the British culture and its style of living. However, her novels lack the warmth and touch of Indianness. Though she has touched upon the theme of human relationships, it is presented within a latticed framework consisting of sophisticated Britishers and learned Indians. She has also delineated women's alienation resulting from the adaptation of British culture by Indians and Indian culture by Britishers. Jhabvala has penned the growing influence of Britishers on Indians which was making them materialistic. While writing about Indians and their families, she has displayed the typical Indian housewives as well as modern, educated women. She talks about the attitude and temperament of Indian women in *Esmond in India* when she writes:

> 'So like animals like cows,' he said with sudden revulsion 'Beat them, starve them, maltreat them how you like, they will sit and look with animal eyes and never raise a hand to defend themselves, saying do with me what you will, you are my husband, my God, it is my duty to submit to my God.' (78)

Jhabvala has given us a glimpse of Indian society in which men hold the place of master and women of slave. The feminine traits inculcated in women force them to unquestioningly submit to their male counterparts. Cultural difference also baffles them. Judy in *A Backward Place*, who has a British upbringing, is unable to cope with an Indian husband, similarly Gulab in *Esmond in India* reticently endures her British husband's callousness. Jhabvala has written about a particular section of Indian society, which thrived soon after India received her independence and has limited herself to a particular time-frame. Her themes do not possess a universal appeal. Her writings too do not become a part of feminist literature as they relate about women and their plight with no aim of ameliorating their pathetic state.

Kamala Markandaya is one of those contemporary writers who have tried to define the pathetic condition of Indian women by raising some feminist issues. She talks about women trapped in their poverty like Rukmani in *Nectar in a Sieve* and Nalini in *A Handful of Rice,* whereas in *The Golden Honeycomb* she has written about women belonging to rich families. Unlike Anita Desai and Ruth Prawer Jhabvala, she points out that the crux of all prevailing problems of women is their financial dependence. Her women characters like Premala, Sarojini, Vasantha and Meera project the idea that the economic independence of women shall solve most of their problems. These characteristics of Kamala Markandaya's female protagonists distinguish them from women characters of other contemporary Indian-English writers. Her women characters refuse to treat men as oracles. Her novels take up some feminist issues and provide a new, strengthened and independent image of women. Unlike other writers, she not only criticises the deplorable status of women, but also wants to guide and encourage them to transcend it. Though she has suggested financial independence as a remedy to the doomed feminine world, yet many other problems concerned with women, such as social conditioning, sexual discrimination, and forced sex remain unanswered. Still, Kamala Markandaya has successfully propounded some feminist ideas in her novels.

Shobha De's fiction deals with the lives of urban aristocratic women. Marriage to them is a convenience for money, social status and physical gratification, rather than having an emotional and psychological attachment. Shobha De portrays women who, while in quest of self-identity, lose their morality. Her female characters are modern, educated, glamorous, ambitious, money-minded and have thirst for physical gratification. They are relentlessly in search of a new life-partner instead of analysing their marital problems, and are doomed by their spirit of romanticism. Her characters do not possess any moral or ethical values the Indian psyche normally associates with marriage. Infidelity is not a sin but a routine activity for them for which they have no remorse. Her novels portray the metropolitan elites, who have bartered values and ideals for superficial lusts—lust for money, physical gratification, success and ambitions. Shobha De's feministic ideas lack Indianness. Her themes propagate the dilution of family ties by women in order to accommodate themselves in better social positions. Though she takes up some problems related with the lives of women, she fails to suggest any substantial or relevant solutions to them. Her novels present a very small section of contemporary society. It can also be mentioned that feminism which was propagated as a revolution to grant equal rights to women in India, is now being influenced by the feministic concepts of western culture. The enthusiasm to ameliorate the condition of women in an underprivileged society often overlooks the difference in the plight of Indian and western women. According to the western feminists, women should attain their individuality within or without the family, whereas Indian women want to seek their individuality while remaining within the institution of marriage. They value their family, as well as their individuality. They normally do not favour fragmentation and dilution of familial/marital bonds. This difference in the temperament of Indian and western women nullifies the adaptation of western feministic ideology in India. Writers like Shobha De represent a small section of Indian women who get misguided and carried away by their emotional undulations and end their marital knots with no regrets.

In this whole scenario the fiction of Shashi Deshpande comes like fresh air, which not only propagates feminist ideas but also advises women to understand their naked selves. Deshpande's novels suggest that women should take cognizance of their weaknesses, overcome them and implement their potential in order to assert their individuality. As a novelist she mirrors the new socio-cultural context of the process of change. Her novels reflect the social realities of Indian life—they also re-evaluate and reinterpret women's status, helping them to reinvent their identity and community positions, norms and values. The themes dealt by Deshpande in her novels possess universality. They do not refer to a particular woman or a particular section of women in the society but are representative of Indian womanhood. As compared to the novels of Anita Desai, Ruth Prawer Jhabvala, Kamala Markandaya and other early writers, we find her fiction giving a more transparent picture of the status of Indian women. She is neither prejudiced against men nor has any partiality towards her female protagonists. She presents the true facet of the modern Indian society in her novels. Supporting the autonomous self-hood for women she suggests that substantial and reasonable methods should be employed to improve their condition. Like Virginia Woolf, she feels that women should be allowed to utilize their talents, and simultaneously they should fulfil their duties towards their families. Like Betty Friedan, she too advocates that women should be equivalent to men and their existence should be noticed as human beings. Like Simone de Beauvoir she traces and exposes the limitations associated with a woman's life from her childhood to womanhood. Deshpande's feministic concerns are different from those of the other contemporary writers. She presents the new image of the Indian woman—who wants to be a wife, mother and daughter, and simultaneously desires to achieve her individuality. Deshpande's novels define the concept of feminism within the context of Indian social milieu.

Deshpande Explores Indian Myths and Stereotypes

In India, women have been given many legal rights by the Constitution, but the realization of these rights at a social level is still a remote dream. Men in general are unable to overcome the attitudes of male superiority the centuries of indoctrination have generated in their psyche. The pace of change in the pathetic condition of women in India has been quite slow. Literature, reckoned as the mirror of the society, is fully alive to the diverse changes taking place in society and is able to draw the readers' attention towards the plight of Indian women.

Deshpande is the one of those few writers who have acknowledged the influence of myths which is responsible for the debasement of Indian women at social level. Not only the domineering status of man, which is often treated as a manifestation of infallible patriarchal authority, but also the archetypes which act like traditional moulds producing their clones, are responsible for the subjugation of women. In her stories and novels, Deshpande has represented the life cycle of middle-class Indian women and drawn the attention towards the fact that archetypes generated by social myths do not permit unhindered growth to women at any stage of their lives. In her novels we find an authentic portrayal of socio-economic factors reducing women to the status of a pawn and producing a sense of rootlessness in terms of the loss of individual personality. Social and religious doctrines give men the claim to absolute authority. Deshpande speaks about the need to develop a different approach towards myths and stereotypes in her work. In her essay, "The Indian Woman—Stereotypes, Images and Realities," says,

> It's not the myths that are the problem; myths are both necessary and relevant to human lives, they come out of some human need. The problem arises out of the characters in myths to stereotypes, in making them a kind of final statement rather than complex questioning characters in whom we find ourselves. (1997)

She is aware of the magnitude and intensity with which the Indians have linked their lives with these myths. They judge their routine lives by the image reflected by these myths about perpetuating the secondary status of woman. Her works clarify the interpretation and appraisal of the conventional traits by Indian society, which enable us to establish correlations between the predicament of women and established social dogmas. A critical evaluation of these myths is rather difficult as they have been organically assimilated in the Indian life style. It is not only the change in the status of women which is necessary, but also the segregation of the myths from the life and rearing pattern of the average Indian man. Deshpande in her essay "The Indian Woman—Stereotypes, Images and Realities," states about the influence of myths in reshaping the life of people which can never be easily avoided:

> Myths condition our ideas so powerfully that often it is difficult to disentangle the reality of what we perceive from what we learn of ourselves through them. In India, myths are perhaps even more powerful, for they have been with us in a long unbroken tradition. Our epics and puranas are still with us and among us, in the stories told to children, in plays, dances, songs, poems, even jokes—and now, most influential of all, in movies. Over the years they have been reinvested, reshaped, regionalised. The myths continue to be a reference point for people in their daily lives and we have so internalised them that they are part of our psyche, part of our personal, religious and Indian identity. (1997)

These myths imposed many restrictions on women and denied them individuality and identity. Deshpande is the only novelist who has broken the image of women as stereotypical mothers. She has projected the innermost recesses of those women's minds who have other interests besides the perennial interests of domesticity. Women have been portrayed in literature as devoted, loving and caring mothers who are the epitome of self-abnegation. Maternity is viewed as the destiny of women and they are exhibited as accepting motherhood as a boon. Deshpande has reflected the unconventional image of motherhood in which maternity is described as a restricting factor. Her female protagonists do not consider motherhood as the only motive of their existence. They do not want to sideline their self-identity and want to live a life with a purpose. The mother-myth is highly responsible for nullifying women's existence as an individual. Deshpande gauges every relationship in the context of the situation and circumstances within which it exists. In her interview to me entitled "The Fiction of Shashi Deshpande: Women's Journey from Self-Effacement to Self-Actualization," she clarifies her idea about the mother-daughter relationship:

> Every relationship depends upon the circumstances on who you are. And I never see that every relationship is same throughout the world. Mother-daughter relationship does not mean that every daughter and mother in the world is same. There are different kinds of mothers and daughters depending upon what kind of a person you and your mother are and your relationship takes a particular pattern. I see people as human beings first. And I see them as mothers, daughters and wives next. We are born as human beings. All these came later. So we try to play these roles but we don't always succeed because it is not possible for us.

While imitating the archetypes, women lose their true selves. The changing approach towards such archetypes is a reflection of the changing social scene. According to her, women must be assessed beyond their roles as daughters, mothers and wives. Nancy J. Hirshmann concludes in *The Subject of Liberty: Towards a Feminist Theory of Freedom* that the social structure has set a definite role for women:

> This construction of social behaviours and rules comes to constitute not only what women are allowed to do, however, but also what they are allowed to be. (11)

However, Deshpande does not portray violent or destructive women characters; rather she advocates value-permanence in relationships. She appreciates the situation where women are identifying, acknowledging and asserting their existence in the midst of the muddle and turbulence of restricting social norms. In her works there is an urge to accept women as human beings and they enunciate the need to develop a realistic and pragmatic approach to the myths which the Indian society has assimilated in it. The analysis of these myths proves that their existence and application in the contemporary modern society is irrational as they have a constricting influence on women's right to freedom and expression. Deshpande has analysed the stereotypes described in the Hindu mythology who have been admired for their patience, endurance and self-abnegation. Her stories *The Inner Rooms*, *The Last Enemy* and *Hear Me Sanjay* are based on anecdotes taken from the *Mahabharata*. Her treatment of Kunti and Amba imparts a human touch to these mythical characters. She describes their feelings, desires, and expectations from the viewpoint of a common woman. According to her, the image of these mythical characters in the scriptures should not be accepted as it has been portrayed. She states that it was Iravati Karve's *Yuganta* which inspired her to write about Amba, Ambika and Ambalika which later led her to analyse other mythical characters too. She mentions in the personal interview:

> So I could see so much in Iravati Karve which I wanted to pursue. So I think really it was Iravati Karve who was my inspiration but I also always like to go beyond the roles and I never see human beings as they are presented to us. I like to have my own views.

Deshpande accepts that the scrutiny of myths shall enable women to explore the causes of the perpetuation of their secondary status and ultimately overcome their conditioning, "Yes, women writers are now exploring the myths and stereotypes, a phenomenon which has been partly influenced by the growing strength of feminist thinking. This has made it possible for us to ask a great many questions; questions which had never been asked before" (*IWSIR*). Her works depict themes expounding women as shaking off their passiveness and declining to remain dormant. She advocates a healthy understanding of one's own naked self as it is and proposes that it shouldn't be hindered by any societal norm or taboo. She prefers active and balanced participation in life. She vociferously deplores the systematic vassalage, the peculiar disadvantages—civil and social—to which women are subjected even in the most sophisticated societies. The constraints of social conditioning trap even the economically independent women. Deshpande has projected the dilemma of those economically independent and educated women who are still wrapped in the indoctrination. She believes that it is education and freedom from the dependence syndrome which can impart the power and vision to transcend their trauma. Saru in *The Dark Holds No Terrors*, Jaya in *That Long Silence* and Indu in *Roots and Shadows* belong to middle class Indian society and are portrayed as economically independent, educated and self-sufficient women, whereas Shakutai and Kalpana in *The Binding Vine* belong to lower middle-class section of the society. They also represent working women struggling with the chauvinistic male society.

Deshpande's women have an optimistic attitude towards life and believe in establishing their self-identity and nurturing healthy relationships. Hence as a writer, Deshpande's protagonists are different from those of the other contemporary writers like Anita Desai, Shobha De, Ruth Prawer Jhabvala and Kamala Markandaya as they want to assert their individuality while remaining within the family frame. Relationships to them are neither a burden nor compulsion, but an important part of their lives. They do not negate familial ties and want to attain individuality within this framework only. As independent, educated human beings, her protagonists have the power to analyse their pathetic state. They are not violent creatures striking an anti-establishment pose. In her interview to me, Deshpande specifies her concept of feminism,

> And certainly my feminism does not mean promiscuity, it is not out of any puritan or moral thing. I don't know that is feminism in any way. It's individual. There are people who are much happier having many relationships. Don't call that feminism. There are some women who want to stick to one man whether he kicks them or beats them. That is her choice. That's her individual choice; don't call that as 'ism.' So I differ from people who feel that feminism means loose morals, feminism means giving up the family, feminism means hating men. No, it's not all that way to me.

Her novels expose sexist biases and discriminations faced by women. Her rational thinking believes in abolishing the said inequality and gender-roles assigned to women, and motivating them to discover their hidden potential. She is aware of the constricting forces of social norms which suppress the female voice in the middle class society. The novelist has highlighted the plight of the middle class Indian women who are carriers of both the ethnic and moral values of Indian society. As educated and modern women, they find a void in their lives and a feeling of incompleteness in themselves due to the dogmas associated with the female world. Their economic independence helps them to analyse their plight and put them on the path of liberation from social and traditional exploitation. This is the unique contribution of Deshpande to the contemporary Indian English literature. Her conceptualisation of feminism and its delineation in her novels is basically Indian. She has taken up the problems faced by average middle class women and has convincingly represented them in her fictional works. As a writer she has exposed the oblivious attitude of the society towards the predicament of women. She points out to Geetha Gangadharan in an interview, "We have women going about with ghunghat on their faces. And women who have no choice even to decide about having children. We have many people who still advocate Sati, who consider dowry a necessity, who count it a loss when a girl is born and profit when a boy is born. It is this abysmal difference that I want to do away with, as a feminist. We all have a certain inherent potential within us, maybe for different things, but we have a right to put it to use" (254). This belief is shared by other feminist writers and critics too. Simone de Beauvoir believes that the societal mores are unfavourable towards the emancipation of women. She states in *The Second Sex*, "As long as complete economic equality is not realised in the society and as long as the mores authorise women to profit as wife or mistress from the privileges held by certain men, so long will her dream of unearned success remain and hamper her own accomplishment" (98).

The novels of Deshpande have stated various factors, which are responsible for women's subjugation and suppression. They are: to rear a girl-child by inculcating feminine traits, gender discrimination—acceptance of being the second sex, traditional system of marriage—leading to an identity-crisis, sexploitation, stifling conventional norms and establishing the monopoly of male dictum. The novelist reflects the strange incoherence manifested by the idea of femininity. The upbringing of girl-children introduces them to their femininity. It is at this stage that they realise the difference of being a girl. Almost all the middle-class Indian girls have to endure the humiliating experience of gender-discrimination which makes them feel inferior to the extent that they sometimes develop revulsion towards their own femininity. They get so terribly accustomed to concealment and suppression that they accept themselves as the weaker sex born to serve and submit. The customs imposing restrictions with the attainment of puberty, and humiliations associated with it add to their frustration. The rudimentary stage of girlhood daubs their psyche with reticence, patience and silence. Deshpande's novels unhesitatingly propagate and prove that the social conditioning is responsible for reducing women to a secondary status in the society. Her work also exposes the complex and complicated system of traditional Indian marriages. These marriages are consummated on the basis of dowry system without seeking the consent of the girls who submit to their parents' decision and accept the proposal without exhibiting any desire, as they have been conditioned to accept marriage as the ultimate goal of their lives. The whole patriarchal system overlooks their existence and marginalises their power of expression. Through her novels, Deshpande advocates a change in the society is required where a girl should be reared up, dealt with and treated as a human being first rather than as a girl or woman always. Women should also refuse to accept the cruelty and discrimination inflicted on them by the patriarchal society. She points out through her themes that the society should consider women as autonomous beings, whose significance and value should be determined without any reference beyond themselves. She states in her essay "No Man is an Island":

> the issue of gender equality, which embraces everything from female foeticide and equal pay to dowry and rape, has to be faced. Those who are afraid that women will turn freedom into license forget that the needs of daily life impose their own restrictions on human liberty. But often there are no limits to cruelty. And cruelty has to be opposed. To be silent is to abet it. (1992)

In most of her stories and all her novels, she has dealt with the institution of marriage and husband-wife relationship. With her feminine sensibility, she has opened up a new vista of man-woman relationship. Again, she has touched and excavated those hidden corners of women's lives which have been ignored by many contemporary writers. Her work concludes that the whole set-up of Indian marriage system neglects the existence of women. They are draped with the cultural ethos to fulfil a destiny which tramples on their authentic rights of becoming and remaining individuals. Her writings are the evaluation of women's status in marital life where they are denied self-expression and are encouraged and appreciated for their self-abnegation and self-denial. A balanced and harmonious relationship between men and women can be established only when they are equals—socially, legally, and economically.

Deshpande believes that by treating women as their subordinate, men are losing a good companionship. On being compartmentalised by the different roles offered to them, women have to suppress their true selves and try to acclimatise themselves to the desires of others. Career-consciousness, self-esteem, diversity of viewpoints, different value-systems become the cause of marital discord. According to the novelist, a healthy relationship between a man and a woman will help them to understand each other in a better way. When forced to live through traditional roles only the socio-psychic conditions of women abet self-effacement, stifling their spontaneity. Still, total self-effacement is unnatural and often generates resistance. Deshpande's female protagonists overcome their marital discord and rediscover themselves after establishing friendly and satisfying relationship with men outside the marital frame. This relationship also helps them to become better human beings. Saru has Boozie in *The Dark Holds No Terrors*, Manju has Guru in *If I Die Today*, Indu has Naren in *Roots and Shadows*, Jaya has Kamat in *That Long Silence* and Urmi has Bhaskar in *The Binding Vine* as friends. In their company they find the freedom to express themselves which was denied to them in some way or the other by their male counterparts. Her protagonists forcefully present the stifling effect of marriage on women as it negates all opportunities to express themselves. The intense desire to give voice to their sufferings, aspirations and ambitions leads women to establish friendly relationship with men. Hence the friendly relationship pursued by the female protagonists outside the family frame is not a desire but rather a compulsion.

Deshpande has also taken up the theme of rape within the institution of marriage. She has revealed the humility and torture endured by women due to the forced sex. The feminine traits inculcated in women restrict them from deciphering their plight. It is the gravest crime perpetrated on women which disturbs their psychological balance and also annihilates their right to their own body. In her stories *It was Dark* and *Intrusion* she has exposed the trauma of forced sex on women. *It was Dark* also sensitively speaks about the devastating repercussions of forced sexual abuse on a girl child. Deshpande explains in the personal interview about this inhuman act perpetrated on women:

> These things came to me out of what I saw around me and I never felt inhibitive because rape is for me the grossest violation of trust between two people. Whether you are in a family or with your husband or even any other man commits a rape it destroys the trust between men and women. It is also the greatest violence because it is not only a woman's body but it is her mind and feeling of her right to have a control on her body which is gone.

Women are shattered when their protector turns into an aggressor. This brutal act not only lacerates their honour but also disintegrates and destabilises their world. Though women's incessant efforts have earned them important positions in various fields, yet they cannot possess the right on their own body and womb. Such bestial acts inflicted on women cannot be solved legally. A total transformation in the perception of the society is required.

Deshpande assertively argues that the present system of marriage does not allow women to identify their true selves, rather it nullifies their existence. She stands forth in defence of one half of the human species, i.e. women, who have been degraded from the state of human beings and almost sunk to the level of social slaves. With no floor of their own to stand on, they develop a feeling of rootlessness. Dependence syndrome makes their lives amorphous because they are not left with any aim to fulfil or pursue. With no destination to reach, they lead a stagnant life. Her novels allow us a glimpse of those women who were denied self-expression by the conventional social modes. The social conventions advise women to follow the archetypes in order to excel in womanly duties. The whole social frame influences the moulding of women's personality as they have been made to follow its dictates since ages.

Deshpande propagates that women should discover themselves and their weaknesses and try to overcome them. She has not only pointed out the social constraints responsible for the exploitation of women, but also castigated women's habit of ensconcing themselves in the convenient role of marriage and projecting themselves as victims. Her female protagonists find themselves entangled in the blind alley of family life. But instead of running amuck after being terrorised by their predicament, they analyse the magnitude of their problems and are ultimately able to take some important decisions about their lives, confronting the patriarchal world with self-confidence. Restoration of self-identity, denial of self-abnegation and refusal to be a passive partner are the final decisions which her protagonists take for controlling their lives. While taking these decisions, they neither transgress nor detach themselves from their family bonds. They believe in the restoration of family ties. Deshpande expounds in her interview to me:

> The family is a very good kind of an institution. Because human beings do need to live among other human beings. We cannot survive alone and we do need to live in a kind of mixed group where people give and take. I think, family is the best we have at the moment. I don't want to give it up. So for me it is very important that any kind of 'ism' which we evolve should not break up a family.

Deshpande is a novelist who has restored the Indian ethics and values in her works. Unlike other contemporary Indian writers who are propagating a militant version of feminism, Deshpande suggests that the true emancipation of women does not necessarily mean antagonism towards men. She points out that women should realise their true personalities by liberating themselves from the social dogmas and not by negating the family life. Her novels present a mature vision which is not prejudiced against men. She points out in the personal interview:

> both men and women have to progress because you cannot have men standing outside and women saying we want this. It doesn't work that way. It should not be a question of what I want. It should be a question of both of us working together to make a better world. (2001)

She accepts that Indian women have emotional ties with their families and it is not possible for them to ignore either their families or associated responsibilities. However, these emotional ties should not weaken her to willingly accept the role of a servile partner. To her, there is no contradiction between total independence of women and a happily married family life. Her work suggests that women can simultaneously pursue economic independence and family life. She believes that the "family and children are the things which most of us have to take into account. We cannot say that I don't care what happens to my family" (2001). Deshpande's writings dissolve all the misconceptions related with feminism and feminists. Her concept of feminism is closer to the realities of the Indian social milieu where women have a desire for socio-economic independence, retaining their preference for permanent relationships and harmonious family life. She points out in an interview given to Lakshmi Holmstrom:

> Feminism isn't a matter of theory: it is difficult to apply Kate Millett or Simone de Beauvoir or whoever to the reality of our daily lives in India. And then there are such terrible misconceptions about feminism by people here. They often think it is about burning bras and walking out on your husband, children, or about not being married, not having children, etc. I always try to make the point now about what feminism is not, and to say that we have to discover what it is in our lives, our experiences. (248-49)

Thus, we can conclude that Deshpande's fiction is different from other writers in the sense that she not only points out and exposes the wounds of the 'second sex,' but also proposes and suggests their remedies. Her themes present an adequate analysis of the contemporary Indian society. The evaluation of her literature concludes that women should actively participate in life and also relish the family ties, because family, as an institution, is essential for their sustenance. She points out that "for most Indian women to live alone is a very hard life" (2001). Her message is that women should flourish, not only as daughters, wives and mothers but also as individuals. As a novelist she excels in possessing deep knowledge of women's psychology and their predicament associated with their suppression. She objectively diagnoses the norms responsible for destabilising the balance and harmony of marital life and simultaneously does not allow any easy escape to her protagonists for their weaknesses.

Shashi Deshpande's Stories: The Saga of Female Suppression

Deshpande defines feminism as a constructive force which in the patriarchal social set-up should emancipate women from their subordinate position without destabilising human relationships and family bonds. Her feministic ideology not only advocates the social emancipation of women by repudiating to submit to patriarchal oppression, but also suggests that women should realize their potential and assert their self-identity. In her stories she has projected the modern, middle-class Indian women who are struggling to overcome their subordinate position in the male-dominated society. Her women have an optimistic attitude towards life and hence solve the predicament of their lives with a hope for a better future. They do not negate the family life. Retaining their identities as wives, mothers and daughters, they finally restore their individuality and assert their true selves.

Deshpande penetrates to the hearts of issues related with women and their lives. In her five story collections, *It Was Dark*, *The Miracle and Other Stories*, *It Was the Nightingale*, *The Intrusion and Other Stories* and *The Legacy and Other Stories*, she has exposed the idealization with which men have glorified women and criticised the patriarchal desire to keep women as subjects to men. Her stories poignantly exhibit that the girl-child is perceived by the society only as a female and not as a human being. She has also illustrated the female trait of self-abnegation which is responsible for the subordinate position of women in husband-wife relationship. Some of her stories describe the pathetic condition of widows in contemporary Indian society. She has also written a few stories on the plight of some women characters taken from the great Indian epic the *Mahabharata*. Hence her stories have been thematically categorised under the following headings:

1. Girl-child,
2. Self-abnegation,
3. Husband-wife relationship,
4. Widowhood,
5. Epic-based, and
6. Psychology of Men.

The chapter discusses and analyses the feministic ideology of Deshpande under the headings mentioned above.

Girl-Child: The Suppressed Gender

Deshpande is the only contemporary Indian writer in English who has depicted girl-child in all her novels. Girl-child is an oppressed being who has to accept the false ideology of the dominating male patriarchy. The feminine traits are inculcated in them since infancy and they are strictly supervised and guided to carry out their domestic roles in order to perpetuate its designs. They are denied the right to create their own images of femaleness. Simone de Beauvoir writes, "the influence of others upon the child is a factor almost from the start, and thus she is indoctrinated with her vocation from her earliest years" (*The Second Sex* 9). Deshpande has exhibited the psyche, thoughts, desires and aspirations of the girl-child which are often sidelined and ignored by the conventional Indian society. Her stories—'Madhu,' 'The Awakening,' 'Can You Hear Silence?,' 'It Was Dark' and 'Why a Robin?' reveal the world of girl-children, their unlimited dreams and aspirations, as well as their trauma of psychological and sexual abuse.

The stories 'Madhu' and 'The Awakening' exhibit the dream of young girls to achieve independence and an identity of their own. Madhu, the eponymous protagonist of the story, is snubbed and lectured by her mother Lalita for neglecting the household work. Lalita's attitude infuriates Madhu and leads to estrangement in their relationship. The friction between Madhu and Lalita increases due to communication gap between them. Madhu feels frustrated by the restrictions imposed on her and also by the fact that her brother Vinay enjoys total freedom of movement. She states, "I have to face this how, what, where, when every day of my life" (*The Miracle and Other Stories* 46). The story however ends with a positive note as Madhu realises her true feelings for her parents when her father has a stroke.

'The Awakening' projects the young girl Alka, who wants to receive higher education in order to escape her constricting circumstances. She is painfully aware of the claustrophobic conditions of her life, "Six of us in one room. The sounds that came from behind the curtain behind which Baba and mother slept. The common toilets. The smell, as if the whole building was one vast sewer" (*The Miracle and Other Stories* 22). Due to her weak financial condition she has to take up the job of a typist. She feels trapped after her father's death and blames him for not being able to achieve a higher standard in life. Her perception of life changes when she discovers a letter written by her father to her elder brother in which he had expressed his guilt for pushing Alka into a job when she wanted to study. She finally understands her father and evaluates his decision objectively. The story concludes with a note of reconciliation with the situation by Alka. She ultimately emerges as a mature person, ready to face the challenges of life boldly.

'Can You Hear Silence?' tells about Megha, the girl who lives in a small house with her parents and two sisters. She longs to have "a room of her own" (*It Was Dark* 35). She resents the whispers which she constantly hears "from the other side of the curtain" (34) where her parents slept. The story ends with the hope that Megha and her sisters will have a room of their own one day.

'It Was Dark' projects the disturbed mental state of a young girl due to the heinous act of rape committed on her. The traumatic episode has benumbed her and she continuously repeats "It was dark" (*Intrusion and Other Stories* 33). Her mother wants her to recuperate from the pathetic state. The mother's act of pulling back the curtains and allowing the sunlight to gush in symbolises the determination on the part of the mother to make her daughter forget the past and begin the life anew. The story exhibits the courage and determination of a mother who has been silently submitting to her husband's sensuous desires, but is not ready to reconcile with her daughter's plight. The theme of sexual exploitation of girls is again taken up by Deshpande in her novel *Come Up and Be Dead.*

'Why a Robin?' is a story about a girl who approaches her mother to know about the bird robin, as she has a home assignment on it. Her mother feels helpless, as she knows nothing about the bird. She helplessly watches her approaching her father to discuss the assignment and feels isolated. Her daughter returns to her on attaining puberty, as she needed her mother's help to understand the biological development of girls about which she was totally unaware. The story ends depicting love and affection being established between the mother and the child.

The above-mentioned stories describe a true facet of the Indian social-system which never allows girls to develop as independent individuals. They are seldom provided enough space to burgeon fully and are often brutally exploited by males to satisfy their libido. These stories illustrate the novelist's ideology that the girls should identify their own true selves. Family support is also essential to transmute their thoughts into action and to help them overcome their predicament. Deshpande states in her essay "No Man is an Island":

> I believe that the family is not a divine sacred institution, but one created by humans for the benefit of all society; and therefore, it should be built, not on the sacrifice of some, but on the co-operation and compromises of all its members. The loud-cry of the new-born is a triumphant assertion of being—I AM. Does a baby girl cry less loudly?

Her stories accurately and inclusively portray different aspects of the life of a girl-child, and suggest that she should be given the opportunity to understand her true self and assert her individuality not only as a girl but also as a human being.

The Husband-Wife Relationship: The Oppressor and the Oppressed

Deshpande has poignantly described the subordinate position of women in husband-wife relationship, which often annihilates their rights as human beings. Through her stories, she suggests that marriage often tethers women to the conventional feminine traits leading to their subjugation, yet she does not believe in annulment of marriage or family bonds. She is an ardent advocate of harmony and human values in family as well as in society. She insists on the treatment of women as companions rather than as subordinates in husband-wife relationship. She has revealed the true picture of husband-wife relationship in the contemporary Indian society in which men play the role of a dictator and aggressor and women oscillate between their traditional and modern roles. Her works also reveal how different moral codes are set for men and women by the society. Her stories—'The First Lady,' 'Intrusion,' 'The Liberated Woman,' 'The Shadow,' 'Death of a Child,' 'The Alien' or 'Ghosts,' 'My Beloved Charioteer,' 'The Valley in Shadow,' 'A Day Like Any Other,' 'An Antidote to Boredom' and 'The Sweet Antidote' depict the theme of husband-wife relationship.

'The First Lady,' in her story collection *Intrusion and Other Stories*, projects a woman who marries a freedom fighter against the wishes of her father who was "a well-to-do man, fond of the good things of life" (6). Using the flashback technique Deshpande tells us how after her marriage she has transformed herself drastically to suit the likes and dislikes of her husband. Her husband is frequently jailed and she has to face all the difficulties alone. She is shocked when her husband decides to adopt celibacy for the rest of his life. Like a traditional wife she accepts his decision but later in her life "her deprivation" makes her "sensitive" (7) towards a disciple of her husband who soon dies in a police encounter. After independence her husband turns out to be a dishonest and greedy politician who always wants to stick to his power and position. It leaves her flabbergasted "the old don't want to dream now and the young men see no vision" (8). Deshpande has illustrated how the role of a reticent, naive and submissive partner leads a woman to frustration and futility.

'Intrusion' is a story about a newly wed couple who are on their honeymoon vacation. They are complete strangers. The woman wishes to know her counterpart before exposing herself to him. She resists every initiative taken by the man to approach her. Later at night he angrily forces himself on her, which fills her with rage, humility and frustration. The intrusion on her body lacerates her privacy. Deshpande in her interview to me comments on the theme of forced sex on women in marital life:

> When I wrote 'Intrusion,' it came to me as a story of a honeymooning couple. That was how it presented itself to me—as the first night of a couple who had not met before. Of course for all Indian men marriage is a marriage [. . .] but for most girls there is a sense of fear because their bodies have been so private until now. [. . .] So for women, there is a lot of withdrawal, nervousness and a fear of exposing their body or letting men have control over their body. But the men never see that and that was how the story came to me that the man is completely unaware of her feelings.

The story depicts the sexual exploitation of women within the institution of marriage. This theme has been elaborately taken up by Deshpande in her novels also.

'The Liberated Woman' is a story about a lady doctor who earns more than her husband. As a result the man's ego is hurt and he becomes sadistic. She suffers from the crass bestiality of her husband while, ironically, a magazine portrays her as 'The Liberated Woman' in its interview. The story exposes the pathetic condition of women who, despite their economic independence, are exploited by the patriarchal society.

'The Shadow' criticises the rigid moral code enforced on women by the traditional society. The story exhibits a husband's cruel attitude towards his wife and her illegitimate girl-child. Not ready to forgive his wife's weakness, he points out, "You made your own bed. Now you have to lie on it" (*MOS* 61). The child puts all her efforts to get the father's love, but fails. The story reveals the existence of dual moral code which differentiates between the sexes and discriminates against women.

'Death of a Child' depicts a protagonist who assertively takes the decision of aborting her third child. Though her husband calls her a selfish woman, yet she sticks to her decision and refuses to become a breeding animal. "Procreation has always repulsed me. I love my two children, but I have never had any milk for them" (*IOS* 45). She feels guilty after the abortion, but the conviction of taking the right decision pacifies her agony. Deshpande has portrayed a woman coming out of her suppressed state and transmuting her thoughts into reality.

'The Alien' or 'Ghosts' describes a woman's longing for her native land and her husband's ignorance of her loneliness. The story narrates the trauma of a young girl who feels isolated in a foreign world, and is unable to find any companionship with her husband. She never discloses her grief to her parents. The protagonist feels as a stranger in the foreign land and constantly watches television as it "kept the silence away from her" (*IOS* 85). This particular story has been published under two titles—'The Alien' in *It was Dark*, and 'Ghosts' in *Intrusion and Other Stories*.

'My Beloved Charioteer' portrays the hollowness of marriage in which a man establishes himself as an arbiter and treats his wife as a slave. The story revolves around Ajji who watches her daughter Aarti lamenting for her dead husband. While mourning for him Aarti neglects even the presence of her daughter. Ajji also recalls Aarti's preference for her father which had sidelined her in her daughter's life. To make her aware of life's realities, Ajji discloses the imprisoning and stultifying details of her married life to Aarti:

> I lived with him for 25 years. I know he didn't like unstringed beans and hated grit in his rice, I know he liked his tea boiling hot and his bath-water lukewarm. And he hated tears. And so when your baby brothers died, I wept alone and in secret. I combed my hair before he woke up because he didn't like to see women with

> stray hair. And I went into the backyard even then because it made him furious to find stray hair everywhere. (*IOS* 58)

He always brought two saris in a year for her in the colours which she always hated. At nights she submitted before his sensual desires. "When he died," Ajji recalls, "I felt like Priti does when the school is over and the bell rings" (*IOS* 59). The story ends with Ajji finally making her daughter realize her responsibilities. It reflects the duality of patriarchal standards which expect women to find fulfilment in sexual passivity and male domination.

'The Valley in Shadow' is a story about a crippled woman who feels like a nonentity in her husband's life. During a vacation to a hill station she recalls her past. She reminiscences how as a child she was hurt by the sympathising eyes of the people around her and how as a young girl she had helplessly watched her parents searching for her groom. When her marriage is consummated she hopes that the man will appreciate her qualities, that he will realise her true internal worth and not limit himself to her physical disability alone. When after the birth of their son her husband snaps all physical contact with her, she realises that he had married her for money. She recalls, "Not just the money my father gave us, but the money I earned each month" (*IWD* 40). She feels drawn towards the man living next to her room in the hotel. Later she feels guilty for her attraction and decides to return home with her family. The story has portrayed a woman exploited by her husband who is absolutely ignorant towards her feelings.

'A Day like Any Other' is a story which reveals that the society encourages different moral codes for men and women. Women are expected to be chaste whereas men easily get away with their extra-marital affairs. The story describes a woman placidly accepting her husband's infidelity, as she did not want to paralyse her marriage by questioning his unfaithfulness. Marriage provided her the needed social status and economic security and therefore she prefers to overlook the existence of another woman in her husband's life. She repels the whole idea and concludes, "This was the only reality, this home they made together, the life they live together, girl? She laughed. What girl?" (*IOS* 83). The husband is brazenly free from any guilt for violating the sanctity of marriage. The story expounds that marriage provides social security to women and therefore they tolerate the infidelity of their male counterparts.

'An Antidote to Boredom' exhibits a woman who is bored of her stagnant and monotonous marital life. She finds that her husband does not notice her existence and she is taken for granted. She develops an inclination towards a man who is a widower and comes to meet his child at the same school where her son studies. Initially she treats her relationship with the man only as "an antidote to boredom, something I enjoyed because of the excitement it brought into the dull routine of my days, the unchanging pattern of my life" (*IOS* 66). She plans to meet the man in her husband's absence who was going to Delhi for a week. With only four days left for her husband to go she finds all her plans shattered when he asks her to accompany him to Delhi. She decides to discontinue her relationship with the man and also realizes that this relationship had imparted an emotional fulfilment to her which was absent in her marriage. She concludes that it "had been no more antidote to boredom, but the best part of my life" (68-69). The story depicts a man's ignorance towards his wife and also illustrates a woman finding her true self in the companionship of another man. Deshpande advocates healthy relationship between man and woman, and believes that a wife can never reveal her true self to her husband because he often sidelines her existence.

'The Sweet Antidote' describes a woman forcing her husband to commit adultery with her maid in order to ensure the smooth functioning of her household chores. When she realizes that the maid was unable to manage the household work properly because of her suppressed sensuous desires, she forces her husband to establish physical relationship with the maid. The theme of the story is quite uncommon and exhibits a peculiar individual case.

The system of traditional marriages subjugates women and leaves them unprotected to their husband's tyranny. Simone de Beauvoir writes: "Marriage incites man to a capricious imperialism; the temptation to dominate is the most truly universal, the most irresistible one there is; to surrender the child to its mother, the wife to husband, is to promote tyranny in the world" (SB 483). Husband-wife relationship has been taken up as a major theme by Shashi Deshpande in most of her stories and novels. She reflects that within this relationship women's identity, dignity and individuality have been sidelined. The stories project that women can be emancipated by challenging and changing the established social doctrines in which men hold the position of the master and women of the slave.

Self-Abnegation: Crisis in Women's Identity

The traditional Indian society does not allow women's lives to expand beyond the roles of daughter, wife and mother. This trait is systematically inculcated in women since their infancy. As girls, they are made to accept the preference for a male child in the family as a norm and are made to adjust to their secondary status. Self-abnegation is highly responsible for the victimization and exploitation of women. They learn to live a life devoid of choices while men are always encouraged to choose. The patriarchal system always encourages them to find fulfilment through traditionally arranged marriages only. Women who want to pursue careers find themselves maladjusted and bruised, as the traditional marriage is based on the continuation of self-abnegation by women in their different socially permitted roles. Hence we can conclude that self-abnegation begets female suppression leading to identity crisis. It is a vital issue projected by Deshpande in some of her stories and has been developed fully in all her novels. Some of her most sensitive stories—'A Wall is Safer,' 'I Want,' 'Lucid Moments,' 'It Was the Nightingale' and 'Stone Woman'—have illustrated this theme.

'A Wall is Safer' shows how self-abnegation leads to self-effacement. Hema, the protagonist, who is a lawyer by profession, has to leave her job to accompany her husband Vasant. She moves away from Bombay to a place where Vasant was involved in research work. Though Hema explains to her friend that as a wife and mother she had no other alternative, yet she is unable to overcome her emotional undulations arising due to suppression of her individuality. Hema concludes, "A wall is safer. With a wall, you can't even see what's on the other side. But suppose the dangers are inside us? What do you do then?" (*IOS* 121) The story illustrates the dilemma of women moving towards identity crisis due to self-abnegation.

'I Want' presents the compulsion of marriage for a middle-class Indian girl. It portrays a woman deprived of the right to choose. Alka, the protagonist, has to repeatedly face the humiliation of parading before prospective grooms—a custom which is still a part of traditional marriages in India. While settling her marriage, her consent is not taken by her parents. Though she is reluctant to marry the boy because of his unreasonable demands, yet she submits to the decision of her parents. Alka is made to understand that for a woman of twenty-seven it was the time, "to forget dreams and compromise for security" (*MOS* 42). Deshpande has projected the same theme in her novel *Roots and Shadows*.

'Lucid Moments' and 'It Was the Nightingale' are the stories which illustrate women liberating themselves from the conventional mores to establish their identity and attain selfhood. 'Lucid Moments' deals with the attempts of a girl to implant the lost identity of women—women who have buried their identity under the frost of self-abnegation in order to take up socially defined roles. The be-all and end-all of women in Indian society is to enter the marital knot and secure a sheltering tree. Sujata, the protagonist, looks after her dying mother and is shocked to know that her mother's existence has been hardly noticed by her since her childhood. Sujata contemplates about those customs and rituals which make men appear high and mighty and at the same time nullify women's existence. Women never are really a part of any family. Sujata feels that after the death of Akka they will forget her existence too. Hence after her death she installs the photograph of her mother in the house to prove "that even if they never chant a litany of their names at a wedding, these women are real?" (*IOS* 79) The story illustrates the changing mindset of women who finally awaken to their suppressed identity in patriarchal set-up.

'It Was the Nightingale' expounds the rejection of feminine traits by the protagonist as she moves ahead in her career to secure a better future. She declares her decision of joining a foreign assignment for which she has to live away from her husband for two years. Since her childhood she has detested the image of her mother who as a woman

> had nothing of her own. Who tried to live her life throughout her husband and daughters? Who was shattered by any tug at the bonds? Who tortured herself and tormented us. Who made her own shell and glorified it. (92)

The story illustrates a woman's efforts to assert her true self and also depicts her revulsion towards self-abnegation. The protagonist restores her self-identity instead of submitting to the marital demands.

'The Stone Women' portrays women moulding themselves on the dictates of their male counterparts. The story depicts a couple visiting a temple "built by King Vishnuvardhana" (*IOS* 142). The protagonist, after watching the sculptures carved on the walls of the temple, finds them unreal as they represented the fantasies of the sculptors. She recalls that she too has transformed herself according to the desires of her husband. When her husband looks at her, it reminds her of stone women. She feels scared of "becoming one of them too, women frozen for all the time into a pose they have been willed into" (146). But soon she reconciles with her situation. She concludes, "It's comfortable, I like it" (146). The story depicts women recoiling into the sheltering tree because of the trait of self-abnegation inculcated in them by the orthodox society, which teaches them to treat their desires as trivial. Social conditioning still has a hold over the psyche of women and restricts them from exhibiting their true reaction.

These stories criticize the feminine trait of self-abnegation which teaches women to sideline their desires and dignity for the welfare of the family. Deshpande has narrated that the patriarchal society has denied women the right to choose and has erased their existence and purpose to live an independent and self-reliant life. Women are socially conditioned to accept their subordinate position in the society.

Widowhood: The Deprived Womanhood

Deshpande has discussed the trauma of widowhood in Indian society through her stories. In earlier times, widowed women were lacerated of all human rights and were made to live a life of solitude. The perpetuation of these inhuman norms segregates them from other women, and restrictions imposed on them confine them to a pathetic life. Deshpande's 'The Cruelty Game,' 'And Then. . .,' 'Rain,' and 'A Man and a Woman' are the stories which present the plight of widows who, even in the contemporary Indian society are subjected to various forms of exploitation and are forced to lead a life devoid of any pleasure.

Deshpande's 'The Cruelty Game' reveals the subtle cruelty which the family members perpetrate against Pramila, a fragile widow, and Sharu, her daughter. After the death of her husband, Pramila comes to live at her father-in-law's house. She perceives Sharu as her only possession. The children of the family receive Sharu with a malicious nonchalance. The women of the family condemn Pramila for taking up a job. She is also criticized for wearing presentable clothes and celebrating Sharu's birthday. Women of the family want her to lead a miserable, lonely life as per the social demands; but in a defiant gesture Pramila finally leaves the house with Sharu to marry her husband's friend. The story delineates the incalculable miseries to which widows are deliberately subjected.

'Rain' projects the trauma of Radha, whose life suddenly plunges into a lonely dejected rut after her husband's death.

Radha's loneliness, trauma, agony and insecurity gradually lead her to an intimate relationship with her cousin. He becomes adamant to marry her and soon their marriage is consummated.

A similar theme is taken up by Shashi Deshpande in her story collection 'It was a Nightingale.' In it a story 'A Man and a Woman' illustrates, Lalita, a widow, who is forced to lead the life of an ascetic by her in-laws. All healthy buoyance is snatched from her, which makes her life stagnant and monotonous. Her deprivation gradually draws her towards her brother-in-law Ajit, who is much younger to her. Lalita feels guilty for establishing physical relationship with Ajit. Manohar, her husband's friend, calms Lalita and suggests marriage as a solution for her crippled life of widowhood. Despite being crippled himself, he proposes to marry Lalita. He concludes: "The Day of Judgement. It comes for all of us at different times. Mine is here now" (*IN* 39).

The Indian social system which is largely tradition-bound does not provide enough liberty to widows despite their economic independence. Their opinions and aspirations have always remained unvoiced. Deshpande suggests remarriage of widows as a viable solution of their plight, as in the contemporary society it alone can provide them a social security and also a means to satisfy their physical needs.

'And Then…?' is another story of Deshpande which speaks about widowhood leading to insecurity and dependence. Ajji, the protagonist of the story is left at the disposal of her children after the death of her husband. She feels that she is "[…] a burden and responsibility" (*IOS* 150) on her son, Vishwa. Manju, her daughter, goes to States despite being aware of the fact that her mother is in need of her. The woman laments, "My Anju, I had cried out and she walked away from me without compunction or pity" (150). Loneliness makes her feel helpless and she moves to Bombay to live with her son and daughter-in-law. Manju's friend Shaku requests Ajji to give a room in her house on rent. Shaku states, "[…] it wouldn't be very inconvenient, for you, would it? I mean, you're all alone now…" (154). Shaku's words infuriate her as they remind her of her loneliness. She however realizes that she is also responsible for her pathetic life. She concludes: "Yet in my anger I know the fault is mine. It is I who have done this to myself" (156). The story ends with a positive note declaring the acceptance of life and the possibility of change in Ajji's attitude.

The stories related to widows depict that the remarriage of widows is still not widely accepted by the middle-class Indian society. This theme forms the backdrop of these stories. Deshpande also dealt with the theme of remarriage of widows in her latest novel *Small Remedies*. She observes through these stories that the widows should not be denied their basic human rights, rather they should be encouraged to live their lives afresh.

Stories from the *Mahabharata*

Some of Deshpande's stories are based on themes taken from the great Indian epic the *Mahabharata*. In India myths have a very strong hold on people's psyche. They serve as guidelines for those people who associate themselves with these myths. Tradition not only perpetuates a phenomenon, it also acts as a witness to history which it chronicles. Deshpande has successfully portrayed the picture of archetypes which Indian society has cherished since ages and given it a modern touch. Her stories 'Inner Rooms,' 'Hear me Sanjay' and 'The Last Enemy' depict the stories from the *Mahabharata*.

Iravati Karve's *Yuganta* motivated Deshpande to write the story of Amba, Ambika, and Ambalika. 'Inner Rooms' describes Amba as the princess of Kashi who is abducted by Bhishma along with her sisters for his younger brother, Vichitravirya, the king of Hastinapur. Amba refuses to marry Vichitravirya as she is in love with Shalva, the king of Saubha. She is sent back to Shalva who refuses to marry her stating, "Bhishma defeated me. You now belong to him. I will be dishonoured if I take you for my wife" (*IOS* 98). She is again returned to Vichitravirya who refuses to marry her because she loves another man. Amba accuses Bhishma for her pathetic state and asks Bhishma to marry her. He also refuses because of his vow of celibacy.

The complex web created by the words of men frustrates and infuriates Amba. She finally immolates herself and decides, "she would sacrifice the pawn herself" (*IW-SIR*). The story underlines the social reality that the ruling sex seeks to maintain and extend its power over the subordinate sex in all circumstances. Deshpande states in her essay "The Indian Woman—Stereotypes, Images and Realities":

> Sometimes it seems to me that words and ideas cannot mean the same to us as they do to men, because what they are really built around is the self-interest of men. Women, let us remember, have not participated in the process of word-making. This is what Amba in my story thinks when she asks: Honour, dishonour, right, wrong—they are all understood in the context of men's lives.

'Hear Me Sanjay. . .' presents before us the mythological figure of Kunti. An unconventional glimpse of her life is provided to the reader with the help of the stream of consciousness technique. Marriage snatches her identity and she totally transforms herself from the girl she used to be into a queen. She accepts Madri as Pandu's second wife. Her soul cries for her son, Karna. She hates herself for Draupadi's trauma, as she had forced her to live as the wife of five men. Her attitude towards Draupadi is ambivalent. She despises Draupadi for being a pampered child, yet also feels happy that she has been brought up in a different manner. The memory of war fills her heart with pain. She looks at victory as a big loss as the war has left no one to celebrate it. Deshpande's portrayal of Kunti is shorn of traditional responses to her as the mother of mythical warriors. She is portrayed as an ordinary woman lamenting the sorrows, griefs and pains associated with her life.

'The Last Enemy' portrays Duryodhana recalling his past while standing in water. Though he is as strong as Arjuna and Bhima, yet no one acclaims his strength and valour. He hates Draupadi for turning Krishna against him and accuses himself of being alive while all his men have died. The story ends with the people searching for him as their "prey" (107) and finally locating him. It illustrates the anguish and trauma of Duryodhana who tries to establish himself as a warrior in the eyes of Pandavas and his ancestors, but fails to prove his worth.

Deshpande has written about these archetypal figures with an almost poetic imagination and deep sensitivity. She concludes that women like Kunti, Draupadi and Amba have been deliberately eulogised so that they can fit in certain predefined archetypes. She states in her interview to me:

> These women have been given a certain kind of role to occupy in those myths and through the years they have become stereotypes. In the myth themselves, they may not be stereotypes, in fact they are not. Even Shakuntala in the original *Mahabharata* is not the Shakuntala of Kalidasa. Through the centuries they have become stereotypes and we have accepted them as they are.

Her stories present these characters as human beings with human feelings and desires. The patriarchal society praises them as the epitome of strength and patience, however as women they find themselves exploited and cheated by a society dominated by men. The stories deftly present a critique of the patriarchal society imposing social standards of femininity on all biological women.

Male Psychology

Deshpande has also portrayed the psychology of men in some of her stories. 'And What's a Son,' 'The Legacy,' 'The Eternal Theme,' 'The Duel,' 'The Victory,' 'The Pawn,' 'The Dim Corridor' and 'Anatomy of a Murder' demonstrate the male way of interpreting and moulding things and also the brutal manner of expressing their superiority over the female.

'And What's a Son' and 'The Legacy' describe the desire of a male progeny by men to carry on the family lineage. 'And What's a Son' exhibits a man bucking his illegitimate child on the shoulder of his dead son. The desire to have a son after the death of his son and his weakness for women make him take this decision. The story depicts a man who, in order to satisfy his sensuality and fulfil his desire to have a son, ignores the social decorum. In the male-dominated Indian society, men get indirect social sanction to transgress the established code of moral conduct.

'The Legacy' exhibits a man approaching a doctor to father "a child for him" (*LOS* 17). The doctor lives with the wife for sometime and then leaves the couple as promised by him. Later in his life the doctor comes to know about the man's death and the family's weak financial condition. Before his death he bequeaths all his property to the boy thinking him to be his son. The lawyer who approaches the woman with the doctor's legacy discovers that the doctor's son had died in early infancy and this was the second child" (LOS 1998: 20). The story exhibits the intense desire of men to have a son for which they can even push their wives to commit adultery.

'The Eternal Theme" describes an old lecherous poet who flirts with girls while attending a conference. The story takes cognizance of the psychology of men who actively indulge in flirting overlooking its effect on young girls' psychology.

'The Duel' exhibits a man's revulsion towards women since he had seen his parents copulating together. He used to consider his mother as "pure and undefiled. Until that night" (*IN* 63). A woman who wants him to write an article about her approaches him. He agrees on the condition that she should indulge in physical gratification with him. She finally approaches the man, but during their intimate moments she remains "totally unconcerned and detached" (65). Later the writer finds it impossible to forget her and visits her house. He is shocked to know that her husband and children had died in a car accident the day before she came to him. The story illustrates the male psyche which sometimes takes revenge on women for egotistic satisfaction.

Another story based on similar theme is 'The Victory.' It depicts the psychological imbalance of a boy who seduces his girl friend in order to take revenge from his father for marrying soon after the death of his mother. His mounting aggression is defused by doing so as he feels victorious over womanhood and his father. The boy's rage is satiated with the thought that he has hurt his father. The story depicts the psychology of those men who in frustration take revenge on women.

'The Pawn' illustrates a man Ramaswami who, while entertaining his friend's guests, develops an inclination for the daughter of the family. After their departure he realizes the futility of his fantasies about the girl's love for him. The story describes a man whose sensitivity and romantic idealism has been hurt by such attempt.

'The Dim Corridor' exhibits an adolescent boy's infatuation with his English educator Miss Smita Rao. His mother accuses Miss Rao for misguiding his son as he gave up his decision of becoming an engineer and wanted to opt for literature as his career. He spends his time in reading novels. Miss Rao feels guilty for not holding back the things even though she knew about her "growing influence on him" (*LOS* 84). She instantly decides to set things on the right track and makes Vinod understand the real facet of their relationship, i.e., of a teacher and a student. She too enjoys the inclination of the boy towards her, but recedes as soon as she realises the future repercussions of their relationship.

'Anatomy of a Murder' illustrates a man who works in a grocery shop and develops an intense longing for a woman customer who belonged to a rich class. He concludes that there was "something clean and transparent about her, like rain water collected in a vessel" (*IN* 53). He watches her enjoying the company of her son and never forgets her joyful smile. One day, while delivering the goods, he reaches her house and finds her alone. To his utter surprise he realizes that he does not even exist for her. In his insane rage he kills her. The story portrays the psychology of a reckless man and his impulsive desire to take control of a woman's life.

Shashi Deshpande's stories portray various aspects of a woman's life. She has also touched upon those themes which normally remain undiscussed within the Indian social context. One of her stories boldly discusses a lesbian relationship. In another story she has taken up the thematic motif of social superstitions and their impact on the mob psychology.

In her five story collections, Deshpande has written about submissive womanhood, the feminine trait of self-abnegation, the pathetic life of widows, restrictions imposed on girl-child and male chauvinism. Her stories can be summed up as revealing the true facet of the contemporary middle-class Indian society which is dominated by men. They expound that the society requires a fundamental change, only then women will be able to enjoy their existence as human beings.

Early Novels:
Exploring Women's Existing Roles

In her stories and novels Shashi Deshpande has exposed and explored the pathetic condition of Indian women who are forced to enact the roles patriarchy has prescribed for them. Her early novels *The Dark Holds No Terrors* (1980), *If I Die Today* (1982) and *Come Up and Be Dead* (1983) can be placed in the category of her exploratory novels. In these novels she has sensitively explored the status of Indian women within the family and the role of social conditioning in their lives. They focus on the problematic aspects of women's lives related with female suppression by males. Like Simone De Beauvoir, Deshpande has revealed various stifling conventional mores and diktats, which affect the normal and natural growth of women since their girlhood. Sheila Rowbotham explains in *Hidden from History: 300 Years of Women's Suppression and the Fight against It:*

> Female oppression was determined by birth, 'like the skin of the black.' The unequal social relationship between men and women meant that men could 'brand' women with 'mental incapacity' and call it 'nature.' Women often accepted men's definition of their 'natures.' (41)

As they are reared up as a subordinate under strict supervision, they consider themselves constrained by the rules of social conditioning which leave a deep impact on their relationship with their male counterparts in later stages of their lives. Deshpande's exploratory novels are an excellent collage of human relationships in which women are exhibited as playing different roles and fighting against the strains of marginalisation. In these novels she has touched the core issue of gender discrimination, as well as the trauma of women playing the role of a passive and mimetic life partner in their marital lives. These factors, which reduce women to the secondary position in society, form the mainstream of all these novels.

The Dark Holds No Terrors

Deshpande wrote her first novel *The Dark Holds No Terrors* in 1980, which is an extended and detailed treatment of her story "The Liberated Woman." The novel remains to be the most sensitive of all her novels. As a novelist, Deshpande has a realistic approach towards human relationships and does not believe in portraying her characters as following the footsteps of the archetypes. She wants people to analyse their relationships and situations and develop a constructive approach towards life. She specifies to Geetha Gangadharan in an interview:

> Undoubtedly my novels are all about family relationships. But, I think, I will go beyond that because the relationships, which exist within the family, are, to an extent, parallel to the relationships, which exist between human beings outside. It is like Solzhenitsyn's "One Day in the Life of Ivan Denisovich." The work depicts just 24 hours in the life of a man. It is so limited and yet so universal. Whether I succeed or not in achieving this depth, I do not know. But surely, when I am writing about the family, it is not just about the family. It definitely does not limit my canvas. On the contrary, that is where everything begins. (252)

Deshpande has portrayed mother-daughter relationship in a different perspective. Many of her stories like "Madhu, Why a Robin?" and "My Beloved Charioteer" have delineated an estranged mother-daughter relationship. Most of her novels also focus on it. The novelist has deftly exhibited the crucial relationship of girls with their mothers, which enables them either to come to terms with the feminine world or revolt against the main tenets of femininity. It is Deshpande's unique contribution to Indian English fiction, which is not coloured by the stereotyped image of mother-daughter relationship. *The Dark Holds No Terrors* exhibits the cruelty of undue gender discrimination of mothers inflicted on the girl-child. Gender discrimination is a significant factor in Indian society. The independence of middle-class girls is often curbed by the demands of unquestioning obedience by their parents. Even as a child, the protagonist of the novel, Saru, is acutely aware of her mother's preference for her brother, Dhruva. Saru cannot tolerate this preference as it does not have any rational basis and is extended to Dhruva simply because he is a boy. Consequently she develops sensitivity towards the discriminatory treatment imparted to her by her family. Saru recalls that there was "always a puja on Dhruva's birthday. A festive lunch in the afternoon and an aarti in the evening [. . .]. My birthdays were almost the same [. . .] but there was no puja" (168-69). Saru finds her mother's inclination towards her brother Dhruva and a nonchalant attitude towards herself as humiliating because they nullify her existence as a human being. Dhruva dies by drowning in water while the children are playing together. Though Saru tries her best to save him, yet all her efforts proved to be futile. She recalls, "Dhruva was swiftly, silently going away from me" (145). After the tragic death of her brother, Saru was deprived of all the rights of a child. She is never forgiven by her mother for the death of her brother, Dhruva. She becomes a prey of her mother's blatant favouritism who could not tolerate the existence of her daughter while her son was dead. Mourning envelops the family and her existence is not noticed. At frequent intervals, her mother reminds Saru of her own unquestioned authority in the house which clearly states that Saru's vivacity or curiosity which does not fit into the traditionally defined role of a daughter shall not be tolerated outside her domain. Saru's father carries on the role of a naive observer whom she describes as "pusillanimous" (143). Saru's mother always checked her whereabouts and often complained about her socialising with her friends. Saru reminiscences about her fifteenth birthday which was special to her as she had received a pair of earrings as a gift from her friend, Smita. After adoring the earrings secretively, Saru feels a sense of superiority and importance. However, she resents the gift given to her by her mother because she realizes that it was not a gesture of spontaneous love, rather it was given out of social compulsions to give her a flamboyant appearance as a young girl. She decides, "So that was it! It was not for me, not to please me and make me happy, but because I should, as a growing girl, have these things to wear [. . .]. I don't want them, I don't want to eat, I don't want anything" (171). As soon as she returned home after a walk with her friends, Nalu and Smita, her mother accused her of neglecting the household work:

> 'Why are you so late?'
> 'We went for a walk.'
> 'A walk? Such a long time? Don't you know it's dark?'
> I rarely brought my friends home, rarely went out with them after school. Whenever I did so, there was always a scene. I felt full of a sullen hatred. I could not find words to express adequately. I kept silent and that enraged her even more.
> 'Can't you talk? Am I so much below your notice? You can talk to your friends for hours, but you can't speak a sentence to your mother. What am I? An enemy?'
> 'Is it such a crime to go for a walk?' I burst out.
> 'Walk? Didn't you think you could have helped me at home? There are the vegetables to be cut, the buttermilk to be churned. When you are working, I never ask for a bit of help. I slog the whole day all by myself. But to go for a walk.' (170)

Saru's memories are replete with desolate seclusion which she has to endure because of being born a girl. She never receives the emotional support, which she required after the death of her brother. Her mother's accusations could never relieve Saru of the sense of guilt and she has to endure the repercussions of it in her relationships with other people also. Unable to escape her mother's authority, suppression and callous attitude, she feels stifled, vulnerable and bewildered. Even her father shows no sympathy towards her. Her mother's constant accusation that she was her brother's murderer begets misery and trauma in her life and destroys her mental peace and harmony. Assailed by her mother's fierce blows of charging words, Saru develops asperity towards her. Saru was bereft of all the happiness of a child, which was the punishment for the loss of Dhruva. She could sense her mother's revulsion towards her existence and notices that her mother "never really cared. Not after Dhruva's death. I just didn't exist for her. I died long before I left home" (32). Devoid of motherly love and overwhelmed by her mother's atrocities, she feels lost. Deshpande has highlighted the problem of gender discrimination prevailing in the middle-class Indian society which lacerates and hinders the healthy development of girls. Women are liberal towards their sons whereas an unduly harsh supervision is imparted to their daughters. Deshpande's work conveys the gross inequalities present in Indian society between the genders. Saru's mother is guilty of unconditionally acquiescing to the gender-based discrimination evident in the society.

Social conditioning is also responsible for the deprived state of women. Girls are brought up in a particular fashion which generates the traits of femininity in them. Saru's mother too, strictly enforces the development pattern traditionally set for girls in her family. Social conditioning is responsible for imparting a subordinate status to women. The major factors of social conditioning, responsible for demarcating limitations on women, are—restriction associated with puberty, inculcation of self-abnegation, imitation of feminine archetypes, and marriage which is perceived as the ultimate goal for women. A woman's life is circumscribed by these factors of social conditioning. Yet Saru's mother cannot be blamed for her own negative attitudes, as her atrocities are committed in her ignorance—she only wants her daughter to follow the prevailing social dictates, taking them as a guarantee of her daughter's safe future. Saru also endures and can not escape her mother's efforts to condition her as a woman. She realizes that being a girl is in every way inferior to being a boy. Her mother's intense concern for her marriage, even in her childhood, puts Saru in dismay. Saru recalls:

> 'Don't go out in the sun. You'll get even darker.'
> 'Who cares?'
> 'We have to care if you don't. We have to get you married.'
> 'I don't want to get married.'
> 'Will you live with us all your life?'

'Why not?'
'You can't'
'And Dhruva?'
'He's different. He is a boy.' (45)

The marriage of girls is of utmost importance to their parents. Independence and self-identity are meant for men. This 'boy-girl syndrome' is perpetuated and rationalized by the educated and liberal middle-class Indian people. Many sections of the society despise the presence of the girl-child in family. The prevalent notion is that the boys are the harbingers of family fortune. Sudhir Kakar remarks in *Women in Indian Society*, "The preference for a son when a child is born is as old as Indian society itself. Vedic verses pray that sons will be followed by still more male offspring, never by females. A prayer in the *Atharvaveda* adds a touch of malice: 'The birth of a girl grant it elsewhere, here grant a son.' (qtd. Das, 1962)" (46). He has further illustrated about *Aitareya Brahman* which like their ancient texts "probably refers much as anything to the economic facts of life when it states flatly that a daughter is a source of misery while a son is the saviour of the family" (47).

Deshpande has presented the results of this indoctrination in an evocative manner through her novels. Saru could perceive the presence of gender discrimination in her family even before the death of Dhruva. The preference which Dhruva received for being a male child benumbed Saru in many ways and generated an inferiority complex in her. Dhruva was considered as the carrier of the family name, while Saru was the property to be possessed by some other person. She was made conscious of the physical beauty of which a girl must take care in order to tie the marital knot. "I was an ugly girl. At least my mother told me so. I can remember her eyeing me dispassionately, saying . . . you will never be good looking. You are too dark for that" (61). Since childhood women are prepared for the marriage which is supposed to be their ultimate destiny. Deshpande has critically analysed the suffering of girl-children who have to eschew their true selves and thus the process of self-abnegation begins at childhood.

Deshpande has also disclosed the trauma of the restrictions associated with puberty. During menstruation girls are treated like pariah and are segregated from the rest of the house and domestic life. Every three days in a month, Saru goes through this process which further strengthens the feelings of insult and humiliation. Saru recalls, "It was torture. Not just three days when I couldn't enter the puja room. Not just the sleeping on a straw mat covered with a thin sheet. Not just the feeling of being a pariah, with my special cup and plate by my side in which I was served from a distance, for my touch was [. . .] pollution. No, it was something [. . .] much worse. A kind of shame that engulfed me" (62). All that is woman comes to her in this instance from her anatomical sex. As a girl grows up, she is made to feel different and conscious about revealing her femininity to the male members of the family. This treatment is also a part of the collective male response towards anything feminine. Saru is advised by her mother, "You should be careful now about how you behave. Don't come out in your petticoat like that. Not even if it's only your father who's around" (62). An aversion to her own femininity is slowly and deliberately encouraged in the child till she cries out in horror, "If you're a woman, I don't want to be one" (63). The physical development becomes a horrifying experience for her. She starts hating her womanliness and despises the people for making her aware of her femininity. Almost all the feminist writers have vociferously presented this aspect of feminine conditioning. Simone de Beauvoir clearly states in *The Second Sex*, "From infancy to puberty the girl has grown: day after day her body was always a present fact, definite, complete, but now she is 'developing.' The very word seems horrifying" (42). She further expounds: "Very often the parental attitude seems to inculcate in the girl a sense of shame regarding her appearance [. . .]. This feeling of shame leads the girl to act awkwardly and to blush incessantly; this blushing increases her timidity and itself involves a phobia" (44-45). The girls are made to feel humiliated and frustrated by their own femininity. Deshpande, too has meticulously exhibited the experiences associated with the physical development of girls in *The Dark Holds No Terrors.* Saru is made conscious of her puberty and womanliness and is unable to transcend the constraints set by her mother for her. Even as an adult she is unable to free her psyche from the traditional mores associated with women of which her mother is a symbol. She analyses the constraints associated with adolescence and puberty and develops revulsion towards them. The novel successfully presents that the social conditioning is responsible for the marginalisation of a girl-child. It moulds her to fit into the conventional roles of daughter, wife, and mother with complacence. Women are encouraged to adopt the prevailing conventional mores and self-identity is denied to them. *The Dark Holds No Terrors* has revealed the factors, which have stagnated women's lives and negated the developmental process in their lives.

Deshpande advocates economic independence for all women in order to survive with dignity in a society which is enamelled by indoctrinations. She considers economic independence of women as the first step towards emancipation. She, however, agrees that economic independence alone cannot resolve all the problems related with femininity emanating from the dependence syndrome, which is highly responsible for their subjugation and suppression. She states in her interview to me:

> Certainly economic independence is the most important. I consider economics as a very strong motivating force in human life. Ultimately everything goes down to money, that's the bottom-line.
>
> But at the same time, it is not enough for women to be educated and women to be economically independent. You understand that the society consists of all kinds of people. So if I liberate myself it is not enough because the world also has to be liberated to allow me freedom to live within it. So that is where the problem lies. Certainly, it is important to liberate oneself. Now all my novels begin with liberating oneself [. . .] but after that you are still living in a society where everybody is not thinking the way you are. It does not necessarily mean that you are going to be free but then you are able to at least take the first step which is for me always the most important step.

Most of the female protagonists of Deshpande's fiction are economically independent, yet like Saru they find themselves trapped by the indoctrination prevailing in the society. Still the economic independence and education help them to set themselves apart from their critical position and analyse it. Consequently they are able to understand their apprehensions and overcome their conditioning. Saru is afraid of repeating the monotonous and faceless life of her mother. The image of the lady doctor becomes a source of inspiration to her. She aspires to achieve that image of confident superiority and self-identity displayed by the lady doctor. Though the fundamental meanings of life are still hazy in her mind, the desire to be more than just a wife and mother leads her to pursue a medical degree. "To get married and end up doing just what your mother did, seemed to me not only terrible but damnable" (140). Saru meets severe retaliation from her mother against her decision of seeking a medical degree. For her mother she remains a responsibility, which cannot be avoided as she is a girl and hence requires dowry to get married. Saru is forced to seek her father's support for her admission to the medical college. For the first time her father is decisively on her side. Later she marries Manohar against her parents' wish for which she has no remorse as she has withdrawn into her own shell. But Saru's problems are further intensified by the chauvinistic attitudinal beliefs of the society which affect the husband-wife relationship too.

There are several women characters in the novel who are displayed as being entangled in the vicious web of marital life due to the dependence syndrome. Women are always judged by their marriage, as this is the destiny, "traditionally offered to women by society" (Beauvoir 148). Saru recalls the faceless wives of Manu's friends who do not register any emotion on their face. Engrossed in their servility they forget about their status, self-identity and self-respect. The only career they have is their marriage and they never look beyond it. Adjusting and compromising, they spend their lives like slaves. They are faceless because after toiling hard throughout their lives and performing duties efficiently, their existence is not even recognized. Saru recalls her visit to a friend of Manu. She describes, "The man sat and talked to us. The woman came in later with trays of food, cups of tea and glasses of water. She came in silently, unobtrusively, like a shadow and went out in the same way, her husband's conversation not interrupted even by a fraction of a second by her presence. He did not introduce her to us, and so stray was the man's disregard of her presence that we ignored her too. We ate our food, sipped the tea and gulped the water as if they had been brought to us by a nameless waiter in a hotel" (58-59). Saru recalls her friend Smita who was an enthusiastic and carefree girl in college, yet moulded herself according to the likes and dislikes of her husband after marriage. Like many other Indian wives she too learnt to acclimatise in the new environment by subjugating herself. Smita's name was changed to Anju after her marriage. Her ignominious dependence on her husband made her timid. Saru criticizes Smita's blindfolded proclivity towards her male counterpart. "Ah! There it is! 'He'! There's always time to do all the things 'he' wants to do, but never anytime for doing the things you want to do. You just tag on to him and drift, a small boat towed by a larger ship." (117). Smita does not have any freedom to spend money according to her desire and asks Saru to lend her some money. The girl who used to spend money lavishly during the college days had become financially dependent on her spouse and was going around with a begging bowl to seek monetary help. She states:

> You know I came here for my nephew's thread ceremony. He gave me just enough to buy a small gift for the boy. But I had to buy a sari for my sister-in-law as well. It would have looked very mean if I hadn't. All the others did it. And four of us, the children and I, staying here for nearly a month. He doesn't understand these things. He takes if for granted. I'm welcome here. Now if I tell him, I've bought a sari as a gift, he'll be furious. So I thought, if you lend me a hundred. (118-19)

Deshpande has portrayed women serving in the background as wives, too insignificant to be noticed as individuals. Saru recollects that she too changed herself according to Manu. She was no exception and the sense of pleasing her male counterpart was present in her psyche too. The desire of pleasing the man is so strong that it drowns the true self of a woman. Saru contemplates:

> Her abnegation to his tastes had seemed wholly natural at first. Now, for the first time, she found herself, waveringly, hesitatingly, making her way back to her real self. I, as I would like myself to be. But hunting for that real self had become rather like a dog scrabbling for a long-buried bone. Piles of earth flew up, but where the hell was the bone? Or, had there never been a bone at all? (124)

Deshpande categorically states that the effects of social conditioning and dependence syndrome are responsible for placing women in the position of a puppet. She believes that women can be their true selves only if they transcend these limitations and use their potential to secure individuality and self-identity. Economic independence provides women the power of expression, which they have to sideline as housewives.

The Dark Holds No Terrors also touches upon the man-woman relationship within and outside the context of marriage. Deshpande believes that marriage sets restrictions on women's life, as they have to suppress their desires and ambitions to keep the marital harmony. Once married, women's lives are always determined, interpreted, and understood with reference to their marriage. Their existence is recorded in terms of the relationships and roles they pursue in their family. On the other hand healthy, friendly relationship with the opposite sex outside marriage is not regulated by the domineering male attitudes and allows women to believe in themselves and thus reactivates their potential and true capabilities. She explains in her interview to me:

> In a marriage relationship, I cannot speak of a man but I certainly can speak of the woman that much of you has to remain unexpressed. Because especially in our society women are expected of certain things which are not to be done or not to be said by women. Or you have to be certain kind of a person. So the real you van-

> ishes. Whenever I see women talking about their past before marriage, when they were children, there is a kind of delight in remembering that person because that is the real you and after marriage the motherhood and wifehood both take away certain aspects of you [. . .] as a wife you conform to a certain model, as a mother, parts of you remain unexpressed [. . .]. I think it is with the other sex that certain parts of you come alive and to me, a relationship with a male without the burden of sex and marriage is a very good relationship.

In *The Dark Holds No Terrors* Saru enjoys her marriage till she achieves recognition and acknowledgement among her acquaintances and people around her. As soon as she surpasses her husband's career, a discordant note occurs. In patriarchal culture, the development of women is restricted as they are acceptable only as men's subordinates. Manu feels jealous of his wife's professional success and his bruised ego turns him into a sadist. Saru, who was too exhilarated with "the dignity and importance" (42) which her image of a doctor imparted to her, was soon assailed by fears and worries. Her professional prestige and consequent social standing threatened Manu. He felt sidelined in the whole atmosphere of family and society. His wife was gradually holding the position of a man in the family, as her financial help was responsible for carrying out their domestic life. Her economic independence and superiority over Manohar become a stigma for her, as the society does not appreciate a woman who is more successful than her husband. A woman's motives, aims and ambitions, which are independent of their married counterparts, are never valued by society because first and foremost it views women as daughters, mothers and wives, who should act as subordinates. Thus any kind of superiority in women, whether it is economic, educational, or social, is treated as a transgression of the established norms. The pleasure of self-representation of desires is denied to women: they are cut off from any kind of pleasure that might be specific to them. Women are always judged first and foremost as women and their success in a profession is always considered secondary to their success in marriage. "Saru also knows that her success in marriage means manipulating and manoeuvring her relationship with her husband according to the socially accepted norms and flaunting it all the time. Her intellect, her achievement, her career, her ambitions—if they make her better than her husband—are the stigmas which she shall have to carry like a dead albatross" (Gaur & Pallavi 76). The role of a supportive family member which is thrust upon a girl by society since her childhood is hard to overcome. Even a highly educated, independent woman finds herself helpless in its presence and throttles her right of free expression. Saru finds to her dismay that there is no change in her status as compared to her mother's:

> my mother had no room of her own. She retreated into the kitchen to dress up. She sat in this dingy room to comb her hair and apply her *kumkum*, she slept in her bed like an overnight guest in a strange place. And I have so much my mother lacked. But neither she nor I have that thing—a room of our own. (135-36)

She finds herself unable to express her emotional undulations and the feelings of being suppressed and humiliated stifle her. Despite being a part of the family, she feels like an alien. In an attempt to keep a socially acceptable face, she never reveals her trauma and mental agony to Manu and thus her silence is easily taken as an indication of her submission. The charm of an independent woman leading a happy and successful life loses its sheen. The age-old conventions of the society do not allow a liberated psyche to a woman. Deshpande's novels convincingly depict how the society repulses women's attempts to define their own life. They scratch and maul the psyche of those who rebel against these established norms, imparting a feeling of guilt to them. Saru realizes through her marriage that only a reticent woman, following the footsteps of her male-counterpart, can be accepted by an average Indian husband. Her own fears are reflected in her speech to the college girls when she ironically comments that inequality in marriage is a guarantee to a placid state:

> Women's magazines will tell you that a marriage should be an equal partnership. That's nonsense. Rubbish. No partnership can ever be equal. It will always be unequal, but take care that it's unequal in favour of your husband. If the scales tilt in your favour, God help you, both of you. (137)

The complex web of the society does not allow a woman to achieve superiority over her male counterpart. Since ages she has been relegated to a secondary place. Women who have internalised the concepts of secondary status since their childhood find it hard to transgress this conditioning—those who transgress it are not socially accepted. Saru cautions the girls:

> Have you girls seen an old-fashioned couple walking together? Have you noticed that the wife always walks a few steps behind her husband? That's important, very important, because it's symbolic. If he is an M.A., you should be a B.A. If he is 5'4" tall, you shouldn't be more than 5'3" tall. If he is earning five hundred rupees, you should never earn more than four hundred and ninety nine rupees. That's the only rule to follow if you want a happy marriage. (137)

Saru's words underline the harsh reality that even an independent woman's destiny is controlled by her male counterpart. The domineering status, which has been granted to him since ages, is hard to dissolve. Deshpande observes that the society must abandon the minefield of femininity and femaleness and approach the questions of female emancipation from a different direction. Saru's education and financial independence fail to curtail her miseries and traumas. Centuries of naiveness have made women diffident. Thus, even after gaining economic independence, they fail to secure an identity of their own. Woman "as a wife; exists to serve the purpose of her husband. All aspects of her life are to be determined by this service role of hers" (Kishwar 10-19). Saru decides to leave her job as soon as she got acquainted with the reason behind her husband's sadistic nature. She knew that it was the only way to save her marriage from total collapse. She states:

> The reasoning was simple, clear and remorseless. It is because I am something more than his wife that he has become what he is. I can go back to being nothing but his wife . . . and yet was I ever that? . . . he may no longer resent me. And then. . . . (78)

But Manu rejects her idea of becoming a housewife, as it was difficult to run the house on his salary alone. Saru is unable to understand the complexity of her life. On the one hand she is not accepted as an economically independent wife who not only provides the bread, but also the butter to her family, and on the other hand she is not permitted to exist simply as a housewife. Thus, in the whole web of husband-wife relationship, Saru has been devoid of the liberty and freedom to think and act, which should be possessed by a human being. Deshpande has exposed the true nature of husband-wife relationship, which is always unquestionably taken as a cohesive social unit of a family by the society. She has pointed out that the society has never taken cognizance of women as equals to their male counterparts. Her novels exhibit that the emancipation of women is related not simply with rejecting the power of men, it also involves the transformation of existing power structures. The picture of devoted housewives has veiled the true image of stifled and pathetic women who want their family to acknowledge their existence as equivalents to men. Deshpande believes that the true self of women can burgeon only in those relationships in which they are free from the domineering and dictating rule of men. Such kind of relationship is seldom found within traditional marriages in the middle-class society, while outside the domain of family life it is considered to be a sacrilege for women. Deshpande views such relationships sympathetically. Saru in *The Dark Holds No Terrors* discovers her true potential in her relationship with Boozie. Her relationship with Boozie, her professional mentor, is that of a student and a teacher. The timely help and guidance of Boozie helped Saru in the beginning of her career. To Saru, Boozie was, "the fairy godfather who could, with a wave of his magic wand, make things easier" (92). Manu never questions Saru for her growing intimacy with Boozie. He even overlooks people's sceptical eyes, which looked at the relationship between Saru and Boozie with contempt. Saru knew about the rumours, which spread like fire among people about her rapid success and Boozie's influence in it. Manu, being a man, received a severe blow to his ego. He develops a sense of inferiority under the impression that he is being sidelined in Saru's life as well as in his family. But neither Saru nor Manu spoke to each other about the growing silence between them. Saru's financial help to the family and his inability to tackle the whole situation turns him into a sadist. Saru's better social position as a doctor destroys their marriage. Saru contemplates:

> And so the esteem with which I was surrounded made me inches taller. But perhaps, the same thing that made me inches taller, made him inches shorter. He had been the young man and I his bride. Now I was the lady doctor and he was my husband. (42)

In her relationship with Boozie, she for the first time experiences the charm of being an equal and not a subordinate and discovers her existence as a human being which was denied to her as a daughter and wife. In almost all her novels, Deshpande has portrayed a male confidant through whom the female protagonist realizes her true capabilities and weaknesses. According to the novelist, such kind of relationship between man and woman gives them a space to discover and accumulate their lost selves. They become better human beings with the power to express their desires and get strength to actively participate in life. Deshpande states in her interview with me about married women:

> Sometimes with the family we are not completely ourselves. Like I said we are continuously restricted by our roles. I am so much the wife and mother here that I may not be able to express myself, my whole self. It's very rare with a marriage partner. With a marriage partner if you are able to do that it's a wonderful marriage. There is nothing like that because then there is a freedom of both friendship and the intimacy of marriage, both combined in that. Many times it is not possible. So it seems to me that a husband cannot be a friend most of the time.

Deshpande advocates a healthy and nourishing relationship between men and women. Within its frame, women are not expected to make the compromises which they have to make as wives. They can exhibit and express themselves without guilt or remorse.

Saru understands Manu's sense of inferiority and wounded male ego which has changed him into a sadist. He attacks his wife like an animal, hurting her with brutal cruelty. Saru does not, and in fact, is not equipped to oppose it initially. In her girlhood she was beleaguered by her mother, who treated her as an undesirable person. Drudgery and self-negation become an obvious part of her life and even after her marriage these memories are present in her sub-conscious mind. Manohar's bestial attitude again leaves her wounds bare and she becomes baffled, petrified and miserable. Saru feels throttled by her fears and worries and finally takes refuge at her father's house. Ultimately the distance from her marital surroundings gives her ample time to analyse her plight and review her relationship with her husband. The novel suggests that in order to remove the clouds of ego, ignorance and emotional undulations, women should analyse their ownself. Saru too is able to understand her traumatic past, which gives her freedom from the phantoms of her deprived childhood. It also grants her a cohesive understanding of the whole situation which leads her to understand the reality. She finally becomes sympathetic towards her brother Dhruva, who was scared of darkness. She realizes that in order to overcome her fears, she has to struggle herself and nobody can help her in doing that. She has to defeat the darkness inside her and not succumb to it.

The analysis of her past helps Saru to understand her true self. She discovers that though her male counterpart was dominating, her mute submission was also responsible for her suffering. Once again she decides to fight against the constricting forces. She realizes: "the terrors are inside us all the time. We carry them within us, and like traitors they spring out, when we least expect them, to scratch and maul" (85). She accepts her mistakes and weaknesses and decides to maintain her individuality in her relationship with Manu. She understands that it was due to her silence, submission and subjugation that Manu inflicted forced sex on her. She recalls her varied experiences and puts them in a proper perspective. She decides:

> My life is my own. . . . Somehow she felt as if she had found it now, this connecting link. It means you are not just a strutting, grimacing puppet, standing futilely on the stage for a belief while between areas of darkness. If I have been a puppet, standing futilely on the stage for a belief while between areas of darkness. I made myself one. I have been whose substance has long since disintegrated because I have been afraid of proving my mother right. (220)

The process of scrutinizing one's beliefs enables Saru to find out the reason behind her suffering. She decides to shun silence and work out the hindrances of her life for betterment. She concludes, "All right, so I'm alone. But so is everyone else. Human beings . . . they're going to fail you. But because there's just us, because there's no one else, we have to go on trying. If we can't believe in ourselves, we are sunk" (220).

In Saru, we discover a spontaneous urge to live a fulfilled life. She repudiated her mother's authority as a child and worked hard to achieve an independent image of her own which was quite different from the faceless image of her mother and the other women around her. Her dreams are realized for a brief span of time in her marital life but again they are shattered by the social expectations and the traditional male psyche. She again finds her standing amidst the dark and horrifying bylanes of life. She re-lives her past in her father's house and while recalling her painful childhood, she is able to judge her present more objectively. Deshpande has given her female protagonists strength and power of reasoning which is conducive to their development and emancipation, both intellectually and socially. They refuse to remain chained to the subordinate roles set by patriarchy. The novel expounds the need to change the established indoctrinations which have obstructed women's development. Deshpande also seems to propagate that a woman has to fight her own battle.

She has very appropriately quoted from the *Dhammapada* in the epigraph of the novel:

> You are your own refuge;
> There is no other refuge.
> This refuge is hard to achieve.

It clearly projects that for sustenance one has to organize and depend on one's own efforts. Thus we can say, that women have to assert themselves in order to have an identity. While doing so they not only have to suppress social dictates but also have to acknowledge their weaknesses and realize their true potential. True analysis of oneself paves way for betterment.

If I Die Today

Deshpande's work looks askance at the patriarchal society, which expects women to assimilate the cherished feminine traits. Her writings enunciate the need to treat women as individuals rather than as possessions. Through her fiction we can ascertain the true facts related with the subjugation of women, which is omnipresent in the middle-class Indian society. Women want to negate the social constraints like gender discrimination, inculcation of feminine traits, sexploitation, and dilution of self-identity but being amenable to the male hegemony and their own secondary status, they are torn asunder by their deprived state. Deshpande believes in healthy human relationship in which both men and women are treated equally. She has analysed the indoctrination with equanimity and does not assail them vehemently. The factors which contribute to the exploitation and suffering of women and deny them the right to exist as human beings have been sensitively delineated by her. Deshpande advises that all the problems related to human life and relationships must be solved pragmatically. Her literary works illustrate that woman should reject the constraints of womanhood. Her novel *The Dark Holds No Terrors* has portrayed Saru engulfed in the traumatic experience of her marital life not only because of her sadist husband but also because of her resolute silence, which makes her endure the humiliation with resignation.

If I Die Today (1982) is developed on the pattern of detective novels and depicts a murder mystery. Despite having a storyline of suspense, Deshpande is able to attract our attention towards the female protagonist Manju, who faces identity crisis as well as disharmony in her marital life. What remains uppermost in our mind is the suggestivity with which the middle-age crisis of women is portrayed by the novelist. Their subordinate position and social fears are responsible for the suppression of their true emotions. The suspense created by the superstructure of the plot in a way heightens our awareness about the identity crisis of women.

Deshpande has presented a picturesque and realistic view of women's lives amidst the chaotic atmosphere of modernity. The story of *If I Die Today* revolves around S.D.M. College and Hospital, established by Sethji and his father. The atmosphere appears serene, yet the doctors who are living on the campus with their families can palpably feel a wave of mystery. With the arrival of Guruji, Dr. Ashok's cousin, things change dramatically in the campus. As a patient of cancer, he comes to him in the last stage of his illness. Guruji easily takes admission into the life of other people who reveal their hidden secrets to him. Different people react differently to Guruji as a person. Manju, the protagonist, recalls Guruji as "horribly frank and open about things" and "an enfant terrible in company" (8). She points out that he possessed "the gift of breaking all barriers, ignoring all formalities and approaching you directly as a human being. That, I think was what made all of us succumb to him finally" (9). Meera, Dr. Ashok's wife, describes Guruji as "a rather peculiar man . . . not married . . . and he stays in their village home like a sadhu or sanyasi or something . . . not really, but like that" (5). Cynthia, a paediatrician, calls him, "a strange person" (26). Guru's manner of penetrating into the mind of people made him suspicious about the death of Prabhakar Tambe, the union leader in the mill of Sethji. In a party organized by Rani, the Dean's wife, Guru openly comments on the suspicious death of the popular union leader:

> What really hurts is this . . . that man escapes the death he really deserved, while better men of so much more use to society, die untimely deaths. (29)

Few days later Guruji dies in his sleep. Many people are suspected as potential culprits who could have perpetrated the murder of Guruji. Tony, the husband of Cynthia, claims to know the murderer. Manju suspects the people around her, including her husband Dr. Vijay. Tony's charging words, accusing the doctors as "Bloody killers, killing a dying man who never did anyone any harm. Complacent bastards? He shook all of you up, didn't he? Guru did. He told me about it" (73), leaves Manju petrified as nobody retaliated his accusations. The whole episode confirmed that Guru was killed by one of the members of medical staff. She concludes, "The conviction had come, not from Tony's drunken, truculent speeches, but from the silences with which his words and accusation had been met" (76).

The whole story takes a drastic turn with Tony's death. The Dean disappears for sometime and finally returns to declare that he has resigned his post. Manju's doubts are pacified when Vidya, the Dean's sister, attacks Vijay outside their home. He is rescued by the people who come after hearing the screams of Manju. Vidya emerges as the culprit responsible for the series of murders in the campus. Brought up by her brother, her whole life revolved around him. She "admired him and looked up to him" (135) and never married. She even persuaded Dean to send his children to the boarding school and "that got rid of Rani too" (135). Vidya, an educated and established professional, turns into a culprit as she was not able to understand and analyse her emotions clearly. Deprived of natural outlets for her love and longings, she becomes a prisoner of her distorted image of life and changes into a maniac. She knew that the Dean, her brother, had suppressed the news that Tambe's death had resulted from the doctor's negligence. Guru claimed to know the reason behind his untimely death. He made the Dean realize and accept his mistake. She was scared of her brother's fate after the exposure of the whole mishap. She found the presence of Guru as horrid to her brother's name, fame and position. His growing intimacy with her brother makes her jealous and finally she kills Guru. Later whoever tries to trace the person behind the murder gets killed.

If I Die Today has an aura of suspense and mystery. While it is a good detective story narrated by Deshpande, it also has many relevant issues concerned with femininity are present. The novelist has exhibited the predicament of married women and their incessant efforts to overcome their pathetic status. Lack of communication in a marriage, extra-marital affairs, man as an arbiter, are some of the issues which the novel takes up successfully. Women are portrayed as stifled and torn asunder by these issues. Their subjugation as subordinates and their resolute silence about it contribute to their sufferings. The constraints of being women are not countered successfully by their education and economic independence and they continue their roles as naive observers. Assailed by fears, worries and doubts, they remain dormant in the family till they decide to eschew their submissiveness. All the female protagonists in the novels of Deshpande want to live a purposeful life. They refuse to live a dependent life without self-identity. Manju, the female protagonist, discovers that she "was almost a redundancy at home" (14), when she becomes pregnant for second time. Communication gap exists in her relationship with Vijay, her husband. Though he looks after her, yet due to the growing silence between them Manju concludes, "It was that detached kindness of a stranger" (43). The growing silence acerbates the relationship between them to the extent that even the altercation loses their existence in the marital life. Manju and Vijay restrict their lives to themselves and leave no space even for quarrels or disagreement. Manju resents her motherhood and blames it for chopping off her feathers of freedom. She has to leave her job of a teacher due to the complexity in her pregnancy which she loathes:

> Motherhood I thought. It's a trap. Keeping you in a cage until you lose the desire for freedom; until you forget what the word "freedom" means. (47)

The novelist points out that the society does not permit women to undertake their maternities in freedom. Some female protagonists of Deshpande's fiction develop alienation towards motherhood because it snatches their liberty. All their efforts converge on the child due to which they have to sideline their desires, aims and ambitions. The female protagonist of the story "The Death of a Child" is a woman who refuses to become a breeding animal. Manju despises her motherhood because of the restrictions it imposes on her. Simone De Beauvoir too considers maternity as an obstacle in a woman's life. She states in *The Second Sex*:

> It must be said in addition that in spite of convenient day nurseries and kindergartens, having a child is enough to paralyse a woman's activity entirely; she can go on working only if she abandons it to relatives, friends, or servants. She is forced to choose between sterility, which is often felt as a painful frustration, and burdens hardly compatible with a career.
>
> Thus the independent woman of today is torn between her professional interests and the problems of her sexual life (386-87).

Deshpande has laid bare this particular aspect of feminine suffering. The crux of Deshpande's approach in portraying her women and their predicament is that the exploitation with regard to sex and gender is a matter of serious evaluation by the patriarchy. Manju is unable to manage her three-year-old daughter. She accuses her husband and governess for spoiling and pampering the child. Her relentless efforts to check her daughter's behaviour and manners prove futile. Vijay criticizes Manju for imposing her guidelines on their daughter. "You want this and you want that! Can't you ever see anyone but yourself? Not even your own child?" (46). Perturbed and shaken, Manju reanalyses her psychological and emotional turmoils throughout the night and makes some important decisions related with her daughter and marital life. The next morning Manju wakes up "full of determination" (49) and decides to meet Cynthia who was a paediatrician.

Manju appears as a woman who examines her situation and the factors responsible for producing disharmony in her marital life. It helps her to break the silence in her relationship with Vijay. She is portrayed as a middle-aged woman who is full of fears regarding her status, purpose, importance and identity in her marital life. Her condition is symptomatic of an average middle-aged Indian housewife who finds that the family is completely oblivious of her existence, desires and feelings. All her services are taken for granted and she does not have any recognition. Manju, however, is able to transcend this crisis by her power of analysis, which helps her to ascertain the true facts responsible for her pathetic state and ambiguous problems. Manju looks at Vijay as a suspect in the series of murders taking place in the campus. Unable to trace the culprit, she decides to talk to him. The fear of Vijay's involvement in the murder haunts her relentlessly. Her discussions with Vijay dissolve the estrangement between them. Vijay states that he couldn't approach Manju because she was always "encased" in her "armour of righteousness" (101). Manju's initiative saves their relationship.

Various facets and shades of husband-wife relationship are visible in *If I Die Today*. Sunita and Dr. Anand comprise another couple who are facing frictions in their marital life. Anand establishes his hold on the family as an arbiter. The decisions in the family are made by him and their acceptance by his wife is taken for granted. Sunita has to endure the domineering attitude of her husband who wants to settle abroad, whereas she wants to look after her mother. She shares her agony with Manju:

> "Anand is so happy at the thought of going back. Can I stay here? Can I break up the family?" She made a gesture of helplessness that moved me deeply. She is so old . . . to leave her here and go, it hurts terribly. I wish. (96)

Sunita represents a large section of middle-class Indian women who accept their subordinate position in the family. Since their childhood, this trait is inculcated in them through various suggestive ways. Even after marriage, men and women are not equivalent. Men's hegemony and women's submission are the cherished norms of the society. Sunita is also a prey to such age-old indoctrinations which encourage women to fit into the expectations of others.

Life of some other couples, Shantha and Dr. Kulkarni, and Meera and Dr. Ashok, exhibit the pain and humiliation endured by women due to the extra-marital affairs of their husbands. Shantha was aware of Dr. Kulkarni's relationship with Rani, the Dean's wife. She reticently tolerates her husband's infidelity and never questions him for breaching the sanctity of husband-wife relationship. In marriage, infidelity is considered as a breach of contract. But the domestic role to which a woman is confined has not guaranteed her an equal dignity. Man easily takes liberty with the established moral code set by the society. Women often respond stoically to the unfaithfulness of their male counterparts. Similarly Meera too silently tolerates her husband's infidelity. She is quite similar to the female protagonist of the story "The Sweet Antidote" in which the wife tolerates her husband's extra-marital affair. Meera too endures Ashok's flirtations with Leena, the nurse. Ashok takes it for granted that being a good wife, Meera will forgive his association with Leena. He treats his relationship with Leena as only "a bit of fun" (80) for which Meera will never give him up. The images of women traditionally constructed by men are a strange composite of qualities. They should be young, beautiful, sacrificing, and passionate—a combination which makes them hopeless victims, passive, docile and timid. Manju is shocked to hear the views of Ashok:

> The whole situation was so stereotyped it was almost a cliché. The way Ashok saw it, I mean. He was the erring yet loving husband, Leena the bad woman, the seductress, the temptress and Meera the good and forgiving wife. Ashok had three of them neatly compartmentalised. And yet there was something wrong, something he had missed out. I thought of Leena's face, Meera's sobs the other day. (80)

The novel underlines a grotesque fact about the social moral code, which has different and opposite standards for judging men and women. The novelist states her interview with me: "different moral codes for men and women continue very strongly even today." Marital norms relegate women to domesticity. Thus marriage becomes their only career and means of existence. The very thought of living beyond the sheltering tree makes them insecure and lonely. Thus they accept their position as subordinates and surrender to the authority of their male counterparts. Comparing the position of genders in marriage, Simone De Beauvoir remarks that a girl is

> given in marriage by her parents. Boys get married, they take a wife. They look at marriage for an enlargement, a confirmation of their existence, but not the mere right to exist, it is a change they assume voluntarily. (1961: 151)

Women are encased by their femininity and secondary status in the marital life. The Indian society is so rigid that often economic independence alone becomes meaningless for them. It is difficult for them to act on their own initiative until and unless the rigid Indian social system is freed from the dominant patriarchal structures. The dilemma of Cynthia poignantly underlines it. She is an economically independent woman, a paediatrician and better placed in a job as compared to Tony, her husband, who is a football coach. Unable to perform the role of "the head of the family" (95) he becomes frustrated. Cynthia points out:

> He had an odd complex too, about my being a doctor. If I'd given up my job and become the pathetically clinging female, maybe things would have gone right between us. (95)

Her situation is quite similar to that of Saru, the female protagonist of the novel *The Dark Holds No Terrors.* She too endures the sadistic nature of her husband who was frustrated by her success. The male desire is to control women and circumvent their assertiveness. Deshpande's writings convey that economic independence is a first step taken by women towards emancipation as it saves them from becoming parasites. Yet it is not enough to liberate a woman from social constraints. Their economic independence liberates them from the dependence syndrome and makes them aware of their capabilities and potential. They do not lead a monotonous and stagnant life whereas they are ready to contribute their talent to the society for its betterment. But the mere combination of legal rights and a job does not constitute a complete emancipation: in today's environment working is not liberty. Social structure has not been modified by the changes in women's condition. World still retains the form given to it by men for their convenience. Economic independence of women is in the process of upsetting the institution of traditional marriage. The public life is man's domain; women belong to the invisible private sphere. Any attempt on the part of women to surpass men socially and economically is never tolerated by the patriarchy. In order to uplift women we require the support of men and change in the established myths and indoctrination.

Another couple, Sumant and Vimala, have to endure criticizing eyes of people around them. They look at their marriage with suspicion. Vimala is working as a nurse when she becomes friendly with Dr. Sumant. His wife, who is short-tempered, commits suicide after a quarrel with him. Society accuses Dr. Sumant and Vimala of killing her in order to get married. Vimala explains, "It was suicide, I swear it was. But people began to talk. Specially when Sumant and I . . ." (64). Even after marriage their past followed them. She states, "We can never leave the past behind us. It follows us everywhere" (64). She has to live with guilt and fear for a crime which has not been committed by her. They can not enjoy their relationship and companionship because of the society, which always condemned their nuptial knot because of their pre-nuptial relationship.

Deshpande has meticulously and intricately woven the different facets of husband-wife relationship in a novel, which is full of suspense. With each couple, a new problem, apprehension, and disharmony in marital life have been outlined. Deshpande's novels have exposed the patriarchal society in which men have moulded all the norms to suit their interests. Even educated and economically independent women can be perceived as suffering due to the established social norms and find themselves in a fix under the domineering status of their male counterparts. Deshpande has given the strength and power to her female protagonists to analyse this pathetic state. They form the corrective models of women who want to be autonomous, assertive, self-willed, and independent without paralysing their family lives. They do not want to negate the family life but want the family and society to acknowledge their existence. Deshpande has discussed this issue in most of her novels.

Come Up and Be Dead

Deshpande is a powerful novelist who has dealt with the realities of female life. Her stories as well as novels showcase her perspective which exhibits the plight of female world and restrictions associated with it. She has delineated the fact that even after a span of half a century of independence, Indian women are still entangled in the turmoil associated with their gender. She has brought her female protagonists face to face with the questions related with their lost self-identity and the effects of social conditioning on their psyche. Each of her novels reflects a new problem of middle-class Indian women, their centres of conflicts, exhibiting a world of stifled lives in different circumstances in which they have to endure the problems related with their work and family. Deshpande's *Come Up and Be Dead* (1983) deals with the theme of mystery and suspense, yet her feministic concerns are visible through her female characters who exhibit various shades of women's lives. She has projected the present-day reality in terms of progress related with women, their role as wage-earner, and the influence of socio-cultural conditioning on their psyche. Her novels are a stimulating assessment of today's Indian women. Kshama, Deviyani, Sona, Mridula and Jyoti Raman exhibit the changing attitudes of women towards life. Most of them, being the working women, face the challenges of family life as well as of working place with virility instead of ensconcing themselves into a comfortable shelter of marriage. As an erudite novelist, Deshpande has exhibited the social concerns and constraints related with the lives of modern women in contemporary society. She has excellently blended the detective story with the feministic ideology in the thematic motifs of this novel which fully explores and presents the potential of women so often sidelined by the chauvinistic society.

The story *Come Up and Be Dead* revolves around a girl's school in which Kshama is the Head Mistress. She brings out many relevant changes in the school by "abolishing some of the old customs" which had "cut off the girls from their real world" (100). The parents, the staff, the board of the Governors, and the students admire her and everything seems peaceful till the dramatic suicide of Mridula Dutta, a student of 10th standard. Sanjay kills Jyoti, the teacher, and Pratap, the brother of the Head Mistress, as he doubts that they may reveal something about the business of prostitution which includes him, as well as many eminent personalities of the town. He also tries to kill Sharmila, his cousin, and Sonali, Jyoti's daughter. Later Dr. Girish attempts to kill Deviyani who is a cousin of Kshama, as she persisted to find out the culprit behind Mridula's death. He discloses about the whole business of placing school girls in prostitution either by temptation or by force. Deviyani is rescued by Inspector Pratap and the novel ends with the arrest of Dr. Girish and Mr. Varma. The latter is a member of the Board of Governors of the school.

The novel can be superficially interpreted as possessing an aura of a detective story as it presents a relentless search for the murderers. However the sub-structure of the novel, in which Deshpande portrays the dilemma of modern, educated and working women who want to utilize their true potential and categorically refuse to lead a dependent life, is more dominant and meaningful and raises various issues related with women, compelling the reader to think seriously about the possibilities of their logical solutions. The novel is quite absorbing as it not only holds the reader's attention with its air of suspense, but also reveals the degeneration of human values in the contemporary urban society of India. The novels of Deshpande always capture the true facet of the Indian society which has set rigid moral codes of conduct and constrictive traits for its women, whereas the men are permitted, even encouraged, to behave in unscrupulous manner by chauvinistic norms. In *Come Up and Be Dead* the novelist has also portrayed a series of women characters who are not ready to succumb to the patriarchal society.

Kshama, the head mistress, is presented as an educated modern woman, securing a good profession and post with a feeling of content. Her hard labour makes her successful in her life. She states, "It's mine. It's my achievement that has got me this" (32). She never "burdened" (207) her parents with her problems. Even while leading the hostel life she "suffered" and felt "terrible" (207) because of her inability to acclimatise herself in the new atmosphere, still she never discloses it to her parents. When her father dies, she expects nothing from anyone as she has full faith in her potential. As a headmistress she abolishes the restricting conventional rules of the school, which did nothing to improve the personalities of the students. She is shocked when the Board of Governors asks her to resign after the mysterious death of her brother Pratap. She dislikes them for associating her with the death of Mridula and Pratap and forgetting her efforts which have brought about remarkable changes in the school. She says to Deviyani:

> What have I to do with the death of that woman? That girl? And Pratap . . . must I be punished because of him? It's not fair. I could have done so much. I could do more for this school in a year than all their Johns in decades. None of them has any imagination and vision. A school is for them just a nine-to-five job. And when are the next holidays? While I . . . It's not fair. (207)

Kshama does not believe in leading a dependent life and thus she pays Deviyani for looking after her house. She faces the Mridula episode bravely and never appears weak and timid. When she hears rumours about Pratap's association with Mridula's pregnancy, she despises his presence in her life and asks him to leave the place.

Deviyani, Kshama's cousin, is a scared character as she had

watched her mother suffering from epilepsy. Though her sister, Sumi, gets married and leads a settled life, yet she fails to overcome her fear of having children suffering from epilepsy. She decides not to get married and looks after her mother and father throughout their life. Deshpande has revealed the child psychology through Deviyani's reminiscences of her childhood. Children feel strong and confident if their parents lead an established and successful life. They see them as motivating force and try to follow their footsteps. Deviyani's childhood denied this self-respect to her. She has no childhood association of which she can boast. When she compares her father with Kshama's father, she finds nothing of which she could feel proud. She recalls Kshama's father as

> a remarkable man, an intellectual, a research scholar, an eminent professor. And mine was . . . poor old man, a failure in life. He never did a thing in his life that could be called an achievement. And whatever he did, he did wrong. (28)

Deviyani was brought up in an atmosphere where not much importance was given to education, independence or improved financial conditions. Everything was taken very casually and thus Deviyani never received any guidance or encouragement to live with any aim or self-respect. After her father's death she shifts to Kshama's house where she is paid for looking after her. Kshama knows that Deviyani was "shamefully untrained for anything" (31). But a change in her personality can be seen when she becomes adamant to find the culprit and to put him behind the bars. She even decides not to submit before Kshama's rage and anger against her conjectures. It is her acknowledgement of the futility of her life which forces her to act assertively in the face of the tragic mishappenings in the campus. She realizes:

> For the first time in years, I had felt a surge of emotion inside me. It was so strange a thing I hadn't realised then what it was. Afterwards I knew it was anger. I was full of anger. I knew then I could be silent no longer. I had to speak. Mridula, Pratap, now Jyoti. (206)

After watching Dr. Girish with his wife and the intimacy between them she comes to know that "she would always be outside that room of human companionship" (216). Deviyani discovers that her mother's illness assailed her with fears and worries and she submitted before them instead of analysing them pragmatically. Her mother was suffering from physical illness but she made herself psychologically ill. She realizes that she misinterpreted her mother's illness and made a wrong decision about her life, "It was not my mother's illness that had kept me out. I had been fooling myself all these years thinking that way. I was the diseased one, not my mother" (216). The analytical approach towards her life leads Deviyani to take some important decisions regarding what was happening around her in the campus. She helps the police inspector by giving him relevant information about Mridula, Pratap, Sharmila, and Bunny, and finally helps in bringing the pieces of the whole puzzle together. Deshpande has always advocated an analytical approach towards life through her female characters. Saru in *The Dark Holds No Terrors* and Manju in *If I Die Today* overcome their apprehensions and develop a correct perspective towards their lives only by opting for a logical and rational approach.

Deshpande has presented another female character, Mrs. Jyoti Raman, as a woman who overcomes her deprived state with sustained efforts and frees herself from the dependence syndrome. Mrs Jyoti Raman, the biology teacher and mother of Sona, appears as a strict woman who treats her daughter harshly. Kshama is unable to understand her attitude towards her daughter, Sona. She contemplates, "How could someone who had such good brains be so stupid about human beings?" (32) Sona dislikes her mother and hopes that she "never becomes one" (43). Sona's refusal to motherhood is the only form of protest she can muster. It reminds us of Saru in *The Dark Holds No Terrors*. Saru too, despises her mother for treating her harshly and hates her for her nonchalant attitude. She despises the image of her mother and works hard to have an independent stand. Sona too finds her mother "dominating" (42) and wishes to stay with her father. She is unable to understand her mother's hatred for her father. Deshpande has analysed the mother-daughter relationship from an angle which is entirely different from its stereotyped image in the Indian society. Her portrayal of this relationship in *Come Up and Be Dead* and *The Dark Holds No Terrors* is closer to truth.

Deshpande reveals the true picture of all relationships. She does not believe in the stereotyped portrayal of human relationships as she feels that in the contemporary society they have no relevance. According to her all human relationships should be judged and perceived as per the circumstances in which they thrive. The friction between Sona and her mother persists due to the communication gap between them. Nobody knows about Jyoti's relationship with her husband. She never reveals it to anyone. Jyoti was sixteen when she got married and was totally unaware about "what went on between man and woman" (161). The knowledge of it "in one night" (161) makes her know "nothing about him, apart from his sexual desires which seemed to her both abnormal and insatiable" (161). But she never talks about it to anyone as "she knew you couldn't scream 'rape' . . . not when it was your own husband" (161). Deshpande has taken up the theme of forced sex on women in her stories as well as novels. Her stories "Intrusion," "It was Dark" and her novel *The Dark Holds No Terrors* reveal the trauma of forced sex on women not only in the society but also within the family. In Indian marital system, young girls' freedom of choice has always been restricted. They are hardly consulted at the time of their marriage and offered to possible suitors. Unable to retaliate they feel stifled. Jyoti finds herself "trapped" (161) within her marriage. Her pregnancy makes her feel "sick" (161) because she can't bear the idea of "something growing inside her" (161) and that too "a part of him" (161). Her sickness lands her into her parents' house. The birth of a daughter rejoices her because she thought that a daughter "was even more her own" (161). Her reluctance to go to her husband shocks her parents. She tells her mother about her pathetic state at which she laughs, saying:

> "Oh, is that all?" She said, "Why, we all go through these things. Men . . . they're made that way. There's nothing we can do about it. We've got to put up with their demands. And you'll get used to it one day. We all do." (162)

Deshpande has projected that mothers want their daughters to lead a sheltered and protective life. In spite of being acquainted with the fact that their daughters are leading an unhappy marital life, they advise them to live within the marital frame. Even in her later novel *The Binding Vine*, Deshpande has portrayed mothers dreaming about their daughters' marriage, though they themselves have led a miserable married life. Vrinda Nabar has also commented on women's desire regarding their daughter's marriage in *Caste as Woman*:

> Of course she'll be happy, I'll tell you that flat; she'll have her own home, produce brat after brat. Forget all her youth as she spins out her life I waddling behind him, a good Indian wife. And she'll long to have sons: they are boons from above. Take it from me that they're proof of God's love. And when all her daughters are suitably grown, she'll marry them off as we've done our own. (97-98)

Jyoti too is unable to transcend this traditional mode of thinking regarding a girl's marriage and finally returns to her husband's house. But all her attempts to compromise with the situation prove futile. Her attempted suicide shocks her husband and ends their relationship. She is sent back to her parents by her husband along with her daughter and "it was he who had decided he wanted to divorce" (162). After getting divorce Jyoti regains all her lost confidence and works hard to complete her education in order to get a better job. Her economic independence helps her to move away from "her silently disapproving family" (162). She is shocked to see Sona pestering to live with her father even when she knows that he is a married man and lives with his children. As Sona is too young to understand her mother's trauma, Jyoti never reveals about her father's bestiality. She is possessive about her daughter as she is the only thing she has. In order to save her daughter from falling into the trap of call girl business which has been gobbling each and every girl that comes in its way, Jyoti decides to leave the place. But before she can move away from the school, she is throttled to death. Inspector Pratap discovers that Mrs. Raman has no friends because she was "a woman who kept to herself" (175). He finds that even her death cannot melt her family's anger. Her brother performs the last rites as his duty but there is "no grief" (175) in him. He concludes:

> It was plain the dead woman hadn't very good relations with her family. But there was no hatred, either. The man seemed just impatient to have done with the funeral and go back home. (175)

Mrs. Raman appears as a strong woman who does not compromise despite being misunderstood and struggles alone to achieve an independent stand. Mrs. Dutta, mother of Mridula, is another woman who is not ready to play the role of a silent partner. Being a gynaecologist by profession, she refuses to succumb to her husband's demand of looking after their daughter. She states, "If you don't care about being home, I'm not going to be here, either, sitting and twiddling my thumbs" (71). After Mridula's death they part with each other as nothing common is left between them, not even their child. Through Mrs. Dutta, Deshpande presents the problems which working women have to face owing to the prevalent notion that the children should be looked after by mothers. The society believes that it is a woman's duty to look after her children and men are relieved from such duties. Deshpande projects that women have been over-burdened by the dual responsibilities of motherhood and professional demands. If these restrictions are not shared by their husbands, it leads to marital discord.

Come Up and Be Dead exposes the limitations associated with women's lives and illustrates their desire to live a complete and independent life. The economic independence alone is not sufficient for their emancipation, because the roles which they have to perform as wives, mothers and daughters, put restrictions on them. It contains strong as well as weak women, trying to liberate themselves from the social diktats. The novel also exposes the prostitution business which is spreading like an epidemic in the society. Young girls are either lured or trapped to accept it as a profession and the people behind the whole scheme earn a lot of money. The novel reveals the exploitation of women and girls not only in the society, but also within the family. As an erudite novelist, Deshpande has revealed various traumatic and pathetic facets of woman's life.

Conclusion

The first three novels of Deshpande explore the world of women and disclose some of the shocking facets of their lives. The stories of these novels revolve around the middle-class Indian families and expose the role and status of women in it as a naive observer and a silent partner. Deshpande has also explored the world of independent women who, despite their economic independence, are unable to liberate themselves from the social constraints and suffer owing to the absence of choices within the patriarchal society. The frustrating and restricting mores make women alienated towards the patriarchy yet due to their social conditioning they recede to their subordinate position. The novelist denounces not only patriarchy as the adversary of women, but also women's propensity to accept the hegemony of men. Women are drained of their individuality because they submit themselves to the diktats of men. The first three novels of Deshpande can be categorised as exploratory novels which explore the conventional mores responsible for the marginalization and exploitation of women in the contemporary male-dominated Indian society, and draw the readers' attention to the emotional undulations of women due to the incoherence in their thoughts and actions. Deshpande advocates healthy human relationships in which women should have the freedom to assert their self-identity. Her first three novels explore and expose the factors, which are responsible for the suppression of women in the contemporary Indian society, illuminating the feminine struggle against patriarchy within specific Indian situation.

Shashi Deshpande's Mature Vision: Measuring Women's Traumas and Follies

The novels of Deshpande are a scathing commentary on the social diktats which benumb and stagnate women's lives particularly in the middle-class Indian society. In her earlier novels *The Dark Holds No Terrors*, *If I Die Today* and *Come Up and Be Dead* she has exhibited the plight of women due to their subjugation which is an outcome of their social conditioning. The social conditioning deprives women of the right of expression and in spite of financial independence they have to play the role of a subordinate in their families. The reticence of women often results in the negation of true companionship between husband and wife. Education and economic independence have not been able to successfully counter and uproot the evils generated by generations of social conditioning—this is particularly evident in the middle-class sections of the contemporary Indian society in which women have to shoulder the twin burdens of tradition and nascent modernism in a restrictive atmosphere. The female protagonists of Deshpande's early novels sensitively present this aspect of Indian womanhood. Deshpande's early novels show how even the educated, economically independent women are stifled by the age-old indoctrinations. Her later novels—*Roots and Shadows*, *That Long Silence*, *The Binding Vine*, *A Matter of Time* and *Small Remedies*—reflect the novelist's mature vision as they not only display the traumas associated with women's world, but also portray their follies and weaknesses as women. Hence she has more pragmatically evaluated women's world in her later novels. Her feminist ideology lays stress on making women better human beings, which is possible only if they objectively evaluate their true selves and potential.

Roots and Shadows

In *Roots and Shadows* we get glimpses of Deshpande's mature vision which gradually spreads in an elaborate form in her other later novels, i.e., *That Long Silence*, *The Binding Vine*, *A Matter of Time* and *Small Remedies*. Though a number of female characters are present in *Roots and Shadows*, only three among them—Indu, Mini and Akka—are prominently presented as three different facets of the trauma Indian women have to go through in their lives. The readers are able to perceive their complete development from childhood to womanhood through various events narrated strategically. The whole discussion and analysis of *Roots and Shadows* revolve around these three women characters. Mini presents the sociological aspect of marriage and dowry system, the character of Akka expounds the trauma of child marriage and Indu, the financially independent protagonist, discovers her true self after analysing her past and comparing it with her present.

Mini, Indu's cousin, is trained to become a perfect housewife since her childhood. Her rearing process annihilates and suppresses all the conceptions related with independence and education. Brought up under strict supervision, she becomes acquainted with the real duties of a girl conventionally cherished by the society. Mini's obedience, silence and submission never allow her to go beyond the rules and regulations set by the family for girls. Mini is the representative of those Indian girls who are looked after as a property to be possessed by some other person. Education and career are not meant for them. Devoid of any aim in life Mini too devotes herself to the domestic life. She is never encouraged by her family members to seek education and opt for career to gain independent stand like the boys in the family. Through Mini, Deshpande has delineated that femininity is inculcated in women by gradual and systematic conditioning. They are not born with these traits, rather they are moulded according to the traditional ethos accepted by the society by a slow ruthless process of conditioning.

Betty Friedan has commented that it is the desire not to live like a parasite and to give a constructive contribution to the world in order to establish individuality and gain self-identity which differentiates human beings from animals and machines. She writes in *The Feminine Mystique* that women should be allowed to give a purpose to their existence because "without such purpose, to evoke their full abilities, they cannot grow to self-realisation. Without such a purpose, they lose the sense of who they are, for it is purpose which gives the human pattern to one's days" (313). Shashi Deshpande's writings too advocate the concept of self-realization in women. Mini, who was devoid of any aim in her life, leads a monotonous and stagnant life. Indu recalls Mini as a child:

> Mini had always been very much of a girl, the way a girl was expected to be, helping the women with small odd chores from a very young age, waiting on her father and brothers and being generally docile. Our worlds had rarely touched. (122)

Mini becomes a replica of older women in her family who were her role models. The novel poignantly projects the status of Indian women in their families where they merely fill up the vacant spaces in men's life. They exist only as subordinates, and never as companions. Women's authority is limited up to the domestic life, whereas men take all the decision about family in which women's agreement is taken for granted. Mini too accepts that a girl's life is devoid of choices. She has to acquiesce to the decisions made for her by others. Indu rebelliously wonders at this attitude of women:

> A woman's life, they had told me, contained no choices. And all my life, especially in this house, I had seen the truth of this. The women had no choice but to submit, to accept. And I had often wondered . . . have they been born without wills or have their wills atrophied through a lifetime of disuse? And yet Mini, who had no choice either, had accepted the reality, the finality, with a grace and composure that spoke eloquently of that inner strength. (6)

Mini becomes a prey to dowry system prevalent in Indian society. Her father Anant is jobless and depends on the cultivation of land the family possesses. He knows that due to the financial crisis, he will not be able to get his daughter married. When Akka promises to pay the expenses of Mini's wedding, he agrees to marry her to a distant relative of Akka who was mentally imbalanced. Indu concludes:

> Behind the façade of romanticism, sentiment and tradition, what was marriage after all, but two people brought together after cold-blooded bargaining to meet, mate and reproduce so that generations might continue? (3)

Marriages are consummated in India after satisfying the demands of the groom's family. It is because of this system that the birth of girls is not welcomed by most of the Indian families. Dowry system is the root cause of the budding of certain other evil practices not only in India, but in some other societies too. Bertrand Russell writes in *Marriage and Morals* that in some countries like Japan, "Prostitution is recognised and respected as a career, and is even adopted at the instance of parents. It is often a not uncommon method of earning a marriage dowry" (102).

Dowry system in India has led to many tragic and untimely deaths of girls and brides. The humiliating position of girls in contemporary Indian society is pointed out by Vrinda Nabar in *Caste as Woman:*

> The ordeal of getting a girl married off has acquired grotesque dimensions in Indian society. Female foeticide/infanticide is among its most tragic manifestations. If the girl survives either of these fates, other horrors await her. The more bizarre consequences of this continuance of a rapacious practice are seen in the suicide of the three young sisters in Kanpur, Uttar Pradesh, who hanged themselves to escape the misery and humiliation of being born in a family, which could not afford to provide them with suitable dowries. They are also seen in the 'sale' of innumerable young Muslim girls to aged Arab visitors who sexually exploit and then abandon them. (162)

Deshpande has exhibited the drawbacks of dowry system which has made the position of girls and their parents pathetic and miserable. Financially weak parents often accept any proposal of their daughter's marriage that comes their way. Mini's lackadaisical face makes it clear to Indu that she finds the match incongruous. But in order to save her father from further complexities regarding her marriage, she poses a semblance of agreement and decides not to show her dislike. Anant is satisfied that his daughter is finally getting married in a financially sound family and is not willing to try for any other better match. He states:

> Another chance? We had to wait long enough for this one. Padmini is past twenty-four now. And there's her horoscope. And the problem of finding a family with a status comparable to ours. And when everything clicks there's the dowry hurdle. What am I to do? Let the girl stay unmarried? (51)

Women are toned to merge their aspirations and desires with those of their family. Mini describes to Indu about the efforts made by her Kakas and Kakis as well as her parents to wheedle and lure boys and their families. Every time they reject her, she feels downcast and blames herself for putting her parents in distress. She wishes to get married at the earliest in order to save her parents from the imbroglio of groom hunt. Indu contemplates on the position of women in India where they have to play the role of reticent daughters and wives and absorb the trends set by their predecessors. She believes that women should assert their individuality. Troubled by Mini's attitude, she contemplates:

> What choices do I have, Indu? she asked me. . . . Millions of girls have asked this question millions of times in this country. Surely it was time they stopped asking it. What choices do I have? Surely it is this, this fact that I can choose that differentiates me from animals. (125)

Through Indu, Deshpande has exhibited the deprived womanhood of India, which is taken as a tool to serve men. The novel also states that women accept themselves as weaker sex and thus look for the convenient security of marriage. In order to achieve equality with men they have to behave and think rationally and eschew their image of docile, delicate and dependent gender. Deshpande not only talks about the social emancipation of women, but also emphasizes their intellectual independence. She wants women to become more rational and stop pitying themselves as weaker sex. Since ages, women have been perceived as delicate objects and related with beauty, whereas intellect and physical strength are considered as men's characteristics. Deshpande's fiction conveys that women should judge themselves as human beings and not as females. Mary Wollstonecraft too believes that women should inculcate strength of mind instead of beauty. She writes in *A Vindication of the Rights of Woman*:

> My own sex, I hope, will excuse me, if I treat them like rational creatures, instead of flattering their fascinating graces, and viewing them as if they were in a state of perpetual childhood, unable to stand alone. I earnestly wish to point out in what true dignity and human happiness consists—I wish to persuade women to endeavour to acquire strength, both of mind and body, and to convince them that the soft phrases, susceptibility of heart, delicacy of sentiment, and refinement of taste, are almost synonymous with epithets of weaknesses and that those beings who are only the objects of pity and that kind of love, which has been termed its sister, will soon become objects of contempt. (9)

In *Roots and Shadows*, Akka represents another facet of deprived femininity in Indian society. As compared to submissive Mini, she appears dominant. However her dominance is not habitual, she has acquired it after the death of her mother-in-law and husband. Akka has been a victim of the evils of child-marriage. She gets married at the age of twelve to a man who is much older than her. Marriage stifles her childhood. The soul of a child withers when she cannot tolerate the scathing sexual advances of her husband. At a very young age, she has to satiate her husband's physical advances. Narmada Atya, daughter of Indu's grandfather, tells Indu about the torture inflicted on Akka after her marriage:

> But I heard twice she tried to run away . . . a girl of thirteen. Her mother-in-law I heard, whipped her for that and locked her up for three days. Starved her as well. The child, they said, cried and clung to her mother-in-law saying, "Lock me up again, lock me up." But there was no escape from a husband then. I remember her telling me before my own marriage was consummated, "Now your punishment begins, Narmada. You have to pay for all those saris and jewels." But my husband was thank God, a decent man. (69-70)

Sexual marital sadism is vividly portrayed by Deshpande. Akka too is a victim of sexual exploitation in her marital life. The violent sexual approaches of her husband make her life miserable. Engulfed by shame, humiliation and fear, she endures everything silently. Her husband is unable to gauge her disturbed mental state. Being a wealthy man, her husband also keeps a mistress. As a married woman, she is expected to bear children. But she faces many miscarriages due to "the kind of life she led" (70). Akka's mother-in-law tortures her for her inability to give birth to a living child. Motherhood in India is considered as an essence of womanhood. Childless women and women without son are looked down upon with contempt. Infertility is not perceived as a physical incapability of women to produce progeny, rather it is considered to be a curse on them. Women like Akka have to endure many atrocities and humiliations. Akka's life becomes pathetic when she has to not only bear the cruelty of her mother-in-law but also the infidelity of her husband. Ironically it is only after her husband suffers a stroke that Akka's life changes. The dependent position of her husband makes Akka dominating and she refuses to grant him his wish to meet his mistress. This refusal cannot be taken as a cruel repudiation of womanly pity. It is simply an action of the suppressed potential and thwarted desires of a wasted life. Akka says to her husband:

> Listen to me. It's my turn now. I've listened to you long enough. She came here. Twice she wanted to see you. She cried and begged to be allowed to see you just for a short while. I threw her out. You'll never see her again. (71)

Since then, Akka learned how to dominate. She finally understands the principle of survival of the fittest and grasps full control of the family in her own hands. Akka returns to her parental home as a rich widow and since then saddles her family members as puppets. As a rich widow, she acknowledges her power over relatives and establishes herself as a dictator. Indu recalls Akka after her death as "ruthless, dominating, bigoted and inconsiderable" (22). Her formidable authority never allows people to peep into her life and understand her. Akka represents those Indian women who are assailed by tortures, humiliations, physical and mental sufferings in their marital life, due to which in the later stage of their lives they become ruthless, callous and unkind, but nothing can atone for the previous wrong done to them.

Indu, the female protagonist of the novel, has an estranged relationship with Akka. She tries to saddle Indu but Indu's strong determination to achieve an independent stand helps her to escape her dictatorship. The elderly women of her family try to inculcate the conventional feminine qualities in her too. As a child she observes them following the same feminine traits which are dictated to her. She promises to herself not to become their replica. She recalls, "I had laughed at them, and sworn I would never pretend to be what I was not" (158).

Though a motherless child, Indu never receives her father's attention. Govind, her father, had opted for an intercaste marriage against the wish of his family. After the death of his wife, he starts living away from them. Indu feels that her father would have acted differently if she had been a boy. Deshpande has exposed the Indian society which considers the rearing of girl child solely a duty of women. Men are more concerned about their son. Indu realizes that it was women in her family who always looked after their daughters. Fathers were always aloof. Not much stress was given on girls' education as compared to the supervision given to the boys. Indu states:

> It was a tradition in our family that girls were left to their mothers, that a daughter was exclusively the mother's business. When his girls were in school, Madhav Kaka had never known what class

> they were in. But Sunil's education was so scrupulously and harshly supervised by him, that Sunil had turned deceitful, with the connivance, of course of his mother. (163)

Customs based on gender discrimination have always given preference to male child. Girls have mutely succumbed to the attitudes of parents who treat the male child as an etoile. This is particularly evident in the Indian society in which the son is taken as a guarantee to a secure future. Vrinda Nabar writes in *Caste as Woman:*

> Discrimination between the sexes in India begins at birth, or even before it. It starts before the child is born, in the mother's womb. None of the conventional blessings showered upon a pregnant woman mentions daughter. (51)

Both Mini and Indu are expected to fashion their personalities according to the pre-set notions. Their femininity becomes a burden on them. Indu is made to feel ashamed of her puberty which perplexes her and makes her conscious of her own body. Indu soon starts to resent her womanhood. Her Kaki reminds her, "And don't forget, she had ended. 'For four days now you are unclean. You can't touch anyone or anything'" (79). She is even advised to follow various rituals to ensure peace and harmony in the family. She accepts that there is no difference between her and Atya or any other woman, as to all of them a life without a husband is a curse. She refuses to participate in superstitious rituals and associated beliefs. She is always criticized for questioning the prevalent diktats and rituals and for being more clever and educated than any other woman in the family. Indu states that her education and intelligence were always thrown at her like an accusation, as if it was a disgrace to be clever, "I had sobbed out my heart to old Uncle one day. And he had said, 'For a woman, intelligence is always a burden, Indu. We like our woman not to think'" (33).

In an interview to Geetha Gangadharan, Deshpande describes her own experience which exhibits some similarity with that of the protagonist Indu:

> The stress laid on the feminine functions, at the cost of all your potentials as an individual enraged me. I knew I was very intelligent person, but for a woman, intelligence is always a handicap. If you are intelligent, you keep asking 'Why, Why, Why' and it becomes a burden. I was quite uncomfortable with my own intellect and at the same time, I was quite proud also. (253)

Indu represents modern, educated, middle class working women with independent mind-set, capable and willing of making independent decisions. She is not ready to follow the social diktats without analysing them. Indu speaks against the traditional mode of finalizing marriages which are not decided on the basis of compatibility. She reminds Madhav-Kaka that while consummating arranged marriages they leave "out that great incalculable . . . human emotions" (99). She knows that a girl opting for a marriage of her own choice is often condemned by the family members. She too is condemned for her intercaste marriage with Jayant. Since her childhood she has perceived women performing their duties blindly. They toil throughout the day and their grueling routine never allows them to recognize their true potential. She is shocked when she finds them moulding their daughters to become better women, and not better human beings with self-identity. She decides not to become their replica and works hard to achieve an independent stand. The success in her life always gives her confidence to assert herself. She also wants to make her marital life a success and to achieve it she unknowingly submits herself to Jayant. She recalls:

> Then I had met Jayant. And I had found that he too expected me to submit. No, not expected. He took it for granted that I would. And I did it, because, I told myself. I loved him. As if that justified everything. As if the word took away the taint from the dead. And remembering now I had surrendered to him, step by step, I realize now, that it was not for love, as I had been telling myself, but because I did not want conflict. The hideous ghost of my cowardice confronted me as I thought of this . . . that I had clung tenaciously to Jayant, to my marriage, not for love alone but because I was afraid of failure. (158-59)

In the early phase of her marital life, Indu discovers an intimate friend in Jayant. Her life circumambulates around Jayant and she transforms herself drastically to suit his likes and dislikes. Gradually she realizes that she has lost her true self. She thinks, "Have I become fluid, with no shape, no form of my own? At that moment a savage truth had stared me in the face . . . without wants there is no 'I' (49). She becomes frightened with the thought of becoming an "ideal woman" (49) who "loses her identity in her husband's" (49). Patriarchy considers self-effacement as the most important quality among women which encourages them to obliterate their true personalities. Vrinda Nabar writes in *Caste as Woman* that the woman moves:

> towards a more specific aim: to approximate the ideal wife. If she performs this role well, she is exalted and praised even by men with allegedly radical views. I have frequently heard such men describe women in the following way: 'She may not be particularly intelligent or interesting but she obviously makes a good wife.' The condescending flavour of such remarks, the implication that being a 'good wife' is the one quality a human ought not to lack, limits the range of a man-woman relationship in marriage. (175)

Indu too unconsciously treads the path of the elderly women of her family which she has always resented. In the process of pleasing her husband she hides her desires and emotions "as if they were bits of garbage" (38). She even submits to Jayant's decision of continuing with her job instead of resigning and concentrating on her writings she is genuinely interested in. He reminds her that they need money as they have a "long way to go" (17). Indu helplessly and unwillingly acquiesces to his decision and continues with her job. She states:

> To go where? I had not asked him. I had quietly gone back to work. Hating it, hating myself. Waking up each day and thinking . . . I can't go on. Feeling trapped, seeing myself endlessly chained to the long dusty road that lay ahead of me. (18)

She defines love as "a big fraud, a hoax, a trap—a process of making one humble and dependent." (173). Love does not become a burden as long as it does not lose its spontaneity, but when it becomes a compulsion or duty it loses its originality. In Indian society it is the duty of a wife to love her husband which often proves fatal for her marital life as it destroys the companionship between them. Vrinda Nabar states:

> There is another difficulty in the way of modern marriage, which is felt especially by those who are most conscious of the value of love. Love can flourish only as long as it is free and spontaneous; it tends to be killed by the thought that it is a duty. To say that it is your duty to love so-and-so is the surest way to cause you to love him or her. (95)

Indu feels stifled when love becomes a trap for her. When Akka summons Indu, she leaves for her parental home as a "welcome reprieve" (18). At her parental home, she relives her past which helps her to understand her present. Indu never discusses about the estrangement in her marital life with her family members because she knows that sympathy and words of advice are meant only for girls who marry according to their parents' wish. Akka dies and bequeaths to her all her possessions. Akka, who had strong aversion towards Indu, finally acknowledges her supremacy over other family members. Atya clarifies, "But your shoulders are strong. Akka knew that" (72). Indu is finally eulogized and admired for her independent stand for which she was condemned earlier. The story of Akka's marital life told by Atya shocks Indu. But also it helps her to sympathize with Akka as a woman and understand the reason behind her waspish and domineering attitude. She decides that she cannot leave her family in lurch after enriching herself with Akka's money. She states to Naren:

> This is my family; these are my people. And yet . . . I hate them. I despise them. They are mean and petty and trivial and despicable. I had always told myself . . . I won't be like them. I won't live like them. And I thought . . . I've got away. But to what, Naren? To what have I got away? Is that any better than this? Is there no more to life than this? Are we doomed to living meaningless, futile lives? Is there no escape? I'm afraid Naren . . . I'm afraid. (159-60)

Indu also contemplates on her relationship with Naren, her old Uncle's grandson. She finds love, care, and appreciation for her in Naren. He is a good listener and a confidant in whom she can confide. She discusses her emotional undulations with him, which were causing catastrophic effect on her psyche. She discloses to Naren the stifling effect of Jayant's demeanour, which looks at women, expressing their passions and emotions, as ugly and shocking. Many times she was repulsed by him for her sensual approaches which fill her with shame. She deciphers her plight: "It shocks him to find passion in a woman. It puts him off. When I'm like that, he turns away from me. I've learnt my lesson now. And so I pretend. I'm passive. And unresponsive. I'm still and dead" (33). The repulsive attitude of Jayant impregnates her mind with the thought that she is an impure woman. She concludes, "So that's all I am, Naren. Not a pure woman. Not a too faithful wife. But an anachronism. A woman who loves her husband too much. Too passionately. And is ashamed of it" (83).

Disturbed by her emotional upheaval, Indu establishes physical relationship with Naren. Her momentary physical gratification or relationship with Naren was not the outcome of sincere feelings, attachment or bondage between them. Indu finds that they have no "lingering feelings" (171) for each other and even the physical relationship fails to establish "new bonds" (171) between them. Still, she decides not to tell Jayant about the infidelity committed by her. She concludes, "For that was not important. That had nothing to do with the two of us and our life together" (187). She knows that there are no genuine and strong feelings of love in her for Naren which may adversely affect her relationship with Jayant. She decides not to disclose her physical intimacy with Naren to him as he might not be able to understand its true nature. She accuses herself for cheating Jayant but simultaneously realizes that she has been cheating Jayant since they got married by hiding her true self and pretending to be what she is not. She contemplates:

> Wronging Jayant? I winced at the thought. But had I not wronged Jayant even before this? By pretending, by giving him a spurious coin instead of genuine kind? I had cheated him of my true self. That, I thought, is dishonourable, dishonest, much more than this, what I have done with Naren. (171)

After analysing her attitude towards Jayant she concludes that she too is responsible for the agony and torture to which she has been subjected. She also feels that her home is a place to which she belongs and so she decides to go back because "to think otherwise would be to take the coward's way again" (186). But simultaneously she takes some important decisions about her life. She decides not to hide her true self from Jayant. She concludes:

> But there were other things I had to tell him. That I was resigning from my job. That I would at last do the kind of writing I had always dreamt of doing. That I would not, could not enrich myself with Akka's money. That I would, on the other hand, pay for Mini's wedding. (187)

The novel ends with a positive note with the hope that Jayant will understand Indu's decisions. The novel exhibits Deshpande's mature vision which has given the female protagonist a definite shape and identity. Since her childhood, Indu has identified herself as a human being first. She wants to attain and assert her individuality in all her relationships. Jayant snaps her habit of making her own decisions after marriage. She feels stifled and flabbergasted when she finds that she is losing her independence to attain which she had struggled a lot in her life. She finally decides to reassert her individuality in her marital life. In *Roots and Shadows*, various issues that cause self-effacement in women are visible. Deshpande has also dealt with other social constraints besides social conditioning, like dowry system and child marriage, which do not allow the burgeoning of a girl's personality. The novel exposes many exploitative trends carried on in the society in the name of tradition, which tear asunder the life of women. In this novel, Deshpande's vision towards the constricting norms of the society appears more mature and fully developed.

That Long Silence

Deshpande believes in the moral, intellectual, and social emancipation of women as well as men—she has no revulsion for men. She believes in healthy human relationships between men and women which must be based on companionship, and not on subordination. Women continue to be the sufferers in almost all the situations they face as the social norms and moral codes have been so framed as to be particularly disadvantageous to them. To bring a revolutionary change in the established norms of the society, men and women have to change and to do so, they need the support of each other. Men have to dilute their ego and women have to eschew the image of weaker sex or deprived femininity. Mindsets need to be changed in order to establish equality between the sexes. The patriarchal society should perceive women beyond the roles of daughters, wives and mothers. Traditional male fantasies have created a particular image of women to suit their interests—submissive, servile, docile and self-abnegating. These fantasies have been translated into reality too, as women have been meticulously trained by the patriarchal family/social system to assimilate them subconsciously. Deshpande believes that a big transformation is required at the social level which will acknowledge women as human beings with souls, desires, feelings, ambitions, and potentials. Simultaneously women should utilise their potentials beyond their domestic lives to assert their individuality. The novel *That Long Silence* observes that the traditional Indian set-up finally blocks all escape routes from conventional social diktats unless women determinedly pursue a purpose in life besides domesticity. Women need to liberate themselves from constraints of 'womanliness' which will erase the existing discrepancy regarding their marginalization. As a writer Deshpande has been acutely conscious of need of self-expression and has expressed desire to establish themselves as better human beings in her critical and expository writings. She states in her essay "Literature and Morality" that it is the writer who gives expressions to the hazardous mental and psychological protests of human beings. She writes:

> But what has remained constant through time and space has been the human consciousness of something that exists beyond this mundane existence, beyond mere survival. The human quest for something that gives meaning to this life, an understanding that there is the possibility of a better existence, that there are better selves concealed within us, that there is a voice that speaks out to us of these things and of right and wrong—if these vague ideas haunt all humans, it is the writer who gives expression to them, the writer who creates another world which carries traces of these ideas, the writer who through literature enables all humans to be aware of this area of their lives.

In *That Long Silence* Deshpande illustrates this concept through the character of Jaya, the female protagonist, whose internalization of the image of deprived femininity constantly hinders her growth and development. She represents those Indian women who want to break the barrier of long silence created around them by male hegemony, stopping them from a holistic participation in life. Jaya is the representative of average Indian womer who are hesitant in developing their potential because their psyche is enveloped by the fear of failure. Deshpande questions the established norms and assertively points out that women should give up their weaknesses and follies.

Jaya, the female protagonist of *That Long Silence*, has to endure an incompatible and traumatic marital life. She is one of those lucky girls whose upbringing is free from social conditioning. She is taught to treat herself as essentially different from other girls. Her name also suggests a victorious woman. Jaya's carefree childhood has become a part of her existence, while her husband Mohan has a traditional male psyche with all its oppressive cruelty and insensitivity. Frictions occur soon. Mohan finds self-abnegation a strength in a woman as he has watched his mother suffering mutely and still carrying out her domestic affairs. In order to save her marital life from total collapse, Jaya submits before the hegemony of Mohan. Their relationship lacks companionship and Jaya is reduced to the status of a subordinate. Instead of love, care, affection and understanding, silence dominates their relationship. Jaya contemplates, "Like the chorus of Greek drama, we were distanced from suffering; for us there was just living—one foot in front of another, until death came to us in a natural form" (4). Jaya realizes that anger makes a woman ugly to Mohan. He expects his wife to be demure and coy. As a child she never controlled her anger and emotional explosions, but Mohan's wary eyes made her keep a check on her emotions. She knows that while obeying her husband reticently she is not carrying out the idealized role of Draupadi, Sita or Savitri; rather she is urging her marital life to move forward without any frictions or tribulations. She concludes, "No, what have I to do with these mythical women? I can't fool myself. The truth is simpler. Two bullocks yoked together . . . it is more comfortable for them to move in the same direction. To go in different directions would be painful, and what animal would voluntarily choose pain?" (11) Gradually the submissiveness and silence strangle Jaya's confidence in her. She learns merely to consent to a decision taken by Mohan. Even if Mohan approaches her to seek her advice, she finds herself perplexed. Assured of her unquestioning obedience, Mohan soon establishes a monopoly over her. Jaya sums up, "To know what you want. . . . I have been denied that" (25). Mary Wollstonecraft too agrees that the strategic planning over the centuries has given men a better place in the society. She writes in *A Vindication of the Rights of Women*:

> Ignorance is a frail base for virtue! yet, that it is the condition for which woman was organised, has been insisted upon by the writers who have most vehemently argued in favour of the superiority of man; a superiority not in degree, but essence; though, to soften the argument, they have laboured to prove, with chivalrous generosity, that the sexes ought not to be compared; man was made to reason, woman to feel: and that together, flesh and spirit, they make the most perfect whole, by blending happily reason and sensibility into one character. (63)

Mohan believes that a wife should be submissive, servile and docile. When Mohan gets entangled in a problem at his office, he decides to move to the Dadar flat till the things settle down. Jaya does not want it but acquiesces reticently in order to avoid any altercation between them. She knows that her consent is not important for Mohan and is taken for granted. Jaya's fortitude pushes her to an unending servitude. Mohan's decision of moving into Dadar flat is preordained which needs no discussion with Jaya. Jaya recalls, "I remember now that he had assumed I would accompany him, had taken for granted my acquiescence in his plans. So had I" (11). The growing silence between the two sequesters them apart leaving no space for emotional attachment or psychological understanding. They start living under the same roof not as a husband and a wife, but as strangers. Jaya concludes, "But the reality was only this. We were two persons. A man. A woman." (8). Jaya wants Mohan to repent for his crime but his response that he did it for the benefit of the family constantly echoes in her soul. She finds it hard to detach herself from the crime committed by her husband. She is unable to decide whether to follow her husband or to break her silence and question him. Jaya knows that her silence inadvertently supports the crime committed by Mohan and is responsible for erasing the proclivity towards each other, making their relationship feeble. She recalls the advice of Vanitamami who had compared husband with "a sheltering tree" (32):

> After so many years, the words came back to me. A sheltering tree. Without the tree, you're dangerously unprotected and vulnerable. This followed logically. And so you have to keep the tree alive and flourishing, even if you had to water it with deceit and lies. This too was followed, equally, logically. But in Saptagiri we had a creeper that was watered and manured assiduously; yet it died of too much water, of white ants in the manure that destroyed its roots. (32)

After her marriage, Jaya had hurriedly adopted the womanly traits as followed by the women of her husband's family. In order to appease him she discarded those traits which could be interpreted as rebellious postures. During her first visit to Mohan's place she learns how well defined a woman's place was in his family:

> I had discovered how sharply defined a woman's role was. They had been a revelation to me, the women in his family, so definite about their roles, so well trained in their duties, so skillful in the right areas, so indifferent to everything else. I had never seen so clear, so precise a pattern before, and I had been entranced by it. (83)

Jaya is able to see the clear line of distinction that was laid between men and women in Mohan's family. Men were totally unaware of women's suppression and self-effacement. Deshpande talks to Lakshmi Holmstrom in an interview about the suppressed anger in women which is very common in Indian society:

> I don't know, whether women have been very successful in concealing their anger, or whether men have simply closed their ears. This theme was very important in *That Long Silence*. The total lack of communication between men and women. For example, Mohan's utter inability to understand his mother's despair. He actually calls it courage. A young critic spoke to me once of the 'tone-deafness' that Indian men have cultivated towards women. And that seems to me exactly right. (249)

In order to please Mohan, Jaya tries to become a replica of the women of his family and forces herself to become an ideal wife and woman. She dedicates all her services towards her family. Although it never gives her total happiness, it saves her from guilt. She recalls how a mistake gave her remorse, and a word of praise gave her happiness. When she goes through her diary, she discovers that her mental and emotional undulations that always duelled in her psyche have no place in her diary. She also realizes that she is living without an aim in her life. Jaya states:

> its essential core had been left out. The agonised cries—'I can't cope, I can't go on'—had been neatly smothered. As also the question that had confronted me everyday—'Is this all?' The biggest question facing the woman of these diaries had obviously been:

> what shall I make for breakfast/ lunch/ tea/ dinner? That had been the leit motif of my life. (70)

Jaya is renamed 'Suhasini' after her marriage. The identity with which she had learnt to live is snatched from her. Rather, she is given a new name and identity, and a new environment, and she has to struggle to cope with it. A chirping, lively and enthusiastic Jaya is transformed into a grave, calm and stolid 'Suhasini.' While performing the roles of a wife and a mother and trying to fit in the expectations of her family, she teaches herself to accept this difference, "And I was Jaya, no, the Suhasini, who was distinct from Jaya, a soft, smiling, placid, motherly woman. A woman who lovingly nurtured her family. A woman who coped" (15-16). The novel projects the Indian women who, while aping the image of ideal Indian wife, adopt self-abnegation. Vrinda Nabar too feels that the practice of changing name after marriage is a very subtle device to change the personality of a girl to de-link her from her past. She writes in *Caste as Woman*:

> In some sections of Indian society, however, it is fairly usual even now for the husband to change his wife's first name as well. Nothing could be more symbolic of feudal ownership than this unambiguous assumption that, with marriage, the woman's entire past becomes separate and unconnected with her married life. Moreover, since a name may be seen as conferring a form of identity, a distinctiveness, such a practice implies that it is the husband's prerogative to obliterate his wife's identity, if he so wishes, and to give her a new one of his own choice. (121)

Segregated from her identity after marriage, Jaya passes her life without any excitement, thrill, motivation or encouragement. She concludes that to wait for the coming moment is the women's destiny. Throughout their life, they wait for a moment which can provide an escape from their monotonous life. Men have been completely unaware of this traumatic and stifling part of women's life, because they have perceived them merging their desires reticently with those of their family members. Jaya points out:

> He did not know what waiting was. He had always moved steadily from one moment to the next. But for women the waiting game starts early in childhood. Wait until you get married. Wait until your husband comes. Wait until you go to your in-law's home. Wait until you have kids. Yes, ever since I got married, I had done nothing but wait. Waiting for Mohan to come home, waiting for the children to be born, for them to start school, waiting for them to come home, waiting for the milk, the servant, the lunch-carrier man. (30)

Jaya finds that women have never been truly appreciated for their servility. Family members do not even notice their existence. Even the modern, educated women in India are fighting to establish a firm status in their families. Jaya discovers that she has no place in her parental family tree because after her marriage she is no longer a part of it. She shockingly discovers that neither her Ajji nor Kakis have their names in the family tree. Such custom is due to the fact that the society considers men to be the carriers of family name. The birth of a son is celebrated as a joyous occasion. Women who bear sons secure high place in the Indian society. In order to save their marital life from total collapse women crave to bear a son. Jaya finds that although her maid's marital life is in total disharmony, yet she has a craving for a male child, "Why give birth to a girl behnji, who'll only suffer because of men all her life" (28). She is reluctant to watch her daughter suffer because of marriage and men, and therefore wants to bear a son. Jaya finds that a boy lionises his status as a son. She remembers Vanitamami's nephew Dilip who in spite of being a wastrel, turns out to be a pampered child and is always treated as an etoile. She recalls:

> But then Dilip always created an aura of success around himself. Even when he failed his matriculation his mother fondly said, 'Our Dilip is a non matric,' making a positive qualification of his failure. (22)

While spending her days at Dadar flat, Jaya contemplates on various facets of a woman's life. She had always wanted to become an established and successful writer. Mohan objects to her stories, as her themes seem to portray their marital life. He wants that instead of writing stories based on marital discord, Jaya should write popular articles on superfluous themes. Jaya accepts it in the hope that it shall impart permanence to her marriage. She becomes scared of penning down the stories that were in her mind because she had been scared, "scared of hurting Mohan, scared of jeopardizing the only career I had, my marriage" (144). Jaya remembers Kamat, her upstairs neighbour, who turns out to be her true friend. In Kamat's company, her true self can blossom. She pours out all her thoughts and desires to him. Silence and subjugation that play a prominent role in her relationship with Mohan are completely absent in her relationship with Kamat. In her interview to me, Deshpande comments on Jaya's relationship with Kamat:

> Jaya is very much aware that with Mohan she is Mohan's wife but with Kamat she is many things. She is that kid Jaya, a rebellious kid, she is a writer; she is a frustrated person who cannot write what she wants to. She can be angry with Kamat. With Mohan she cannot be angry because he does not like it.

Jaya recalls that it is Kamat who turns out to be her professional mentor. He acts as a teacher, a guide, and never spares her writings that were full of flaws. Jaya's problems are gradually curtailed by her frequent discussions with Kamat. Though a good listener, he always condemns Jaya for her weaknesses. She is amazed to see that a man and a woman can reveal themselves before each other without feeling guilty. Jaya recalls, "There had been an ease in our relationship I had never known in any other. There had been nothing I could not say to him. And he too. . ." (153). He asks her to overcome her inanities if she wants to succeed in her profession. He points out that she must overcome her complexes and stop posing as a deprived woman who has to toil like a slave, as this attitude was preventing her from pouring out her true self. Kamat points out, "Spare me your complexes. And you're a fool if you think I was joking. I'm warning you—beware of this 'Women are the victims' theory of yours. It'll drag you down into a soft, squishy bog of self-pity. Take yourself seriously woman. Don't sulk behind a false name. And work—work if you want others to take you seriously. This scribbling now and then" (148).

Kamat wants her to overcome the whining attitude and attain a positive assertiveness in her behaviour. He criticizes Jaya for making her family a scapegoat for her failure as a writer. He points out that in reality she was "Scared of writing. Scared of failing" (148). Jaya's relationship with Kamat could have solved her puzzled marital life if he had remained alive. During one of her visits. Jaya finds him lying dead in his flat. Instead of paying her last tribute to him, she runs away out of fear of social criticism for maintaining intimate relationship with a man outside marriage. Deshpande has revealed the conservative norms of the society that always permit only those relationships to a woman which follow the socially ascribed rules. A married woman is morally bound to her husband only. Friendly relationships with other men are not permissible and are looked down upon with contempt. Deshpande on the other hand supports healthy human relationships. She states to Lakshmi Holmstrom in an interview:

> But yes, I did bring in Kamat to serve a purpose: to show Jaya the kind of relationship that she could achieve with a man. She gets a kind of companionship with Kamat that she never gets from her husband. Yet that is marriage and this isn't.
>
> But perhaps I do realise that kind of relationship, the kind of companionship that is possible, although it is very rare. Often it is missing, because of the predominance of the sexual motif in India, within marriage. (247)

By recalling her past in her Dadar flat, Jaya is able to develop a proper perspective towards her life. She rearranges the different fragments of her life after carefully analysing her past. She understands herself not only as a wife and a mother, but also as Jaya. She realizes that she has bucked her failures on Mohan's shoulders. Even after Mohan's objections, she continued with her writing. But the publishers rejected them all. She now admits that her writings have been perfunctory and she has been rejected as a writer because of the loopholes in her writings, Mohan has no concern with it. Jaya accepts that instead of improving herself as a writer, she has been accusing her family for throttling her talent and ability. She realizes that she had decided to transform herself according to the desires of Mohan and that made her feel that he has staggered her development. Jaya concludes:

> I hadn't stopped writing because of Mohan; I could not possibly make Mohan the scapegoat for my failures, for I had written even after that confrontation with him—stories that had been rejected, stories that had come back to me, stories that I had hidden here in this house. (145)

With this thought she comes to understand the problems related with her marital life. Jaya realizes that she has to erase the darkness from her soul and mind that is responsible for creating emotional frictions. She understands that as the presence of light overcomes darkness, she can remove the darkness of her mind and soul by analysing her true self. Jaya has never negated family life. Now she realizes the value of leading an organic life. She learns that her fear of failing as a wife and mother has seized her independent thinking. She now decides to move forward in her life expecting a change in Mohan's attitude. She knows that it is not easy to change oneself but she hopes that she can develop a better understanding with Mohan as a companion, rejecting the traditional silence of a wife. All her emotional turmoil is pacified and she concludes, "I'm not afraid anymore. The panic has gone. I'm Mohan's wife, I had thought, and cut off the bits off me that had refused to be Mohan's wife. Now I know that kind of fragmentation is not possible" (191). Jaya appears confident as all her fears vaporize. The novel ends with her resolve to break her long silence. Jaya concludes, "But we can always hope. Without that life would be impossible. And if there is anything I know now it is this: life has always to be made possible" (193). The novel presents Deshpande's belief that women should assert their potential to achieve self-identity. It also shows that economic independence is an important measure to give women a confidence, helping them to preserve their true selves. Deshpande is aware of the tensions which Indian women have to face in order to make compromises between their professional and personal lives. Jaya represents the commonest compromise available to a woman. As a person, as a novelist, Deshpande states that women should not try to escape the challenges of their professional life. In her interview to me, she comments:

> To be a professional, you have to give a lot of yourself. That is where the problem lies, really, because you have to be ruthless. Like Jaya begins by saying you have to be ruthless. You cannot have it all. So you have to give it 100%. Now that is where women really falter. And for that there are a lot of reasons, we are soft, brainwashed, our families come first, genuinely we want to give our children more attention. The solution is not to have children and marriage but that is not possible. For most Indian women to live alone is a very hard life. So each one of us is trying to find one's own way [. . .]. We all have to make compromises. To me it is important that I would never compromise on my professional excellence that I should give my best [. . .]. But the family and children are facts which most of us have to take into account.

Deshpande's *That Long Silence* is a scathing critique of Indian marital system which obstructs the free communication and expression of women. *That Long Silence* not only exposes the prevalent patriarchal practices of feminine marginalization, but also illustrates how their psychology has been toned by centuries of conditioning. Women unconsciously imbibe and follow the image of ideal womanhood, which in fact they have always resented. The novel also reveals how women try to hide their weaknesses and follies behind the façade of deprived femininity. Deshpande believes that women cannot be emancipated socially and legally until they give up their despondent attitude towards life. The main determinant of their success is their ability to assert their individuality. They have to give a purpose to their lives—desultory attempts will never emancipate them from social diktats and conditioning. Deshpande's literary works give us an image of true Indian womanhood—who discovers her true self while remaining attached to the bond of care, affection and admiration that she has developed for her family. The idea that women can achieve their self-identity without negating family life is Deshpande's unique contribution. Women must inculcate a determination to transcend social diktats and overcome their own weaknesses. Deshpande's mature vision is reflected in her later novels in which she has presented her female protagonists' assertive and clear views about life, family, relationships and self-identity.

The Binding Vine

The Binding Vine meticulously projects the strongly knit bonds of human relationships in Indian society. The novel suggests that the individual differences of opinion, emotional frictions and disagreements can never dilute these bonds because nobody can lead an isolated life. This idea is true within the Indian context where close family ties and human bonds provide hope, motive and reason to live. Beneath this superstructure, the story of the exploitation of women within the family is continuously present as a strong undercurrent. To the middle-class Indian women, familial relationships are substantive and can never be negated, but at the same time they also become prey to the conventional norms associated with the institution of marriage. The novel attentively and precisely exhibits the plight of women due to the suppressed and submissive roles they have to perform within a middle-class family—human bonds are like creepers which are wound around them leaving no exits or escape routes. Deshpande suggests that cultural norms should be reinterpreted to make them comfortable for women. A woman definitely needs man but as a person she also desires to preserve her independence and freedom. She talks about the whole complex network of human world in an interview to Uma Mahadevandasgupta:

> I only know that to love, to be loved, are as important as the basic urges. The world is a strange and frightening place, sometimes cruel. When we slip into it, we are physically connected to another human being by the cord. The desire for a connection never leaves

> us, I guess. And apart from the individual desire, there is a universal human instinct to connect, the sense that we are not complete in ourselves, that there is something more of us, that we are part of a large entity. "No man is an island. . . ." Yes, indeed, it's true. (1)

The desire to possess and be possessed is the basis of various human relationships. *The Binding Vine* projects the complex web of relationships in which women adjust and compromise with the most humiliating and exploitative trends of the society. The novel poignantly presents the plight of Indian women who have been self-abnegating and self-effacing themselves—their desires and independent stands—at every stage of their family life to fulfil their social obligations. Women have to bear a social stigma throughout their lives if their marriages are not successful. Consequently they prefer to endure the trauma of marriage and family, which perpetuates their emotional, physical and sexual exploitation. Women, who are toned and conditioned to accept family as a sheltering tree and marriage as the only motive for their existence, fail to exhibit their defiance towards the suppressive norms of the patriarchal society. Deshpande has exposed the suppression and exploitation of women within the institution of family. Women characters of the novel—Shakutai, Mira, Sulu and Kalpana—exhibit the worst kind of physical and mental exploitation to which women can be subjugated by men. Shakutai has no control over her own life in the early phase of her marriage. After her marriage, she comes to Bombay and discovers that her husband is out of job and stays with his cousin-brother who is working in police. They welcome her as she is an easily available servant who never asks for a salary. Shakutai accepts all the challenges of her life boldly and courageously, but is shattered by the humiliation which she has to face by sleeping in the common passage outside their room. Urmi, the female protagonist, perceives Shakutai's fierce rage when she states, "I, a woman, had to sleep there in public, with strange men walking up and down. And my husband . . . the voice drops low 'you know what men are, he wanted to . . . We're not animals, I told him. As if he cared. And I got pregnant" (110-11). The novel vociferously projects the harrowing experiences of rape committed within the precincts of marriage and family. Women are expected to fulfil several duties as wives, one of them is to satiate the sensual desires of their male counterparts. Simone de Beauvoir also accepts that society considers physical gratification as a duty of women towards their counterparts. She states in *The Second Sex:*

> even the primitive societies that are not aware of the paternal generative role demand that woman have a husband, for the second reason why marriage is enjoined is that woman's function is also to satisfy a male's sexual needs and to take care of his household. These duties placed upon woman by society are regarded as a service rendered to her spouse: in return he is supposed to give her presents, or a marriage settlement, and to support her. (149-50)

Like physical gratification, motherhood is also often imposed on women. Most of the Indian women never prepare themselves for it, or plan to become mothers. Consequently motherhood becomes a burden on them. To acclimatize in a new environment after marriage in itself is a difficult task for women; sudden arrival of pregnancy deteriorates their condition further. Shakutai too feels perplexed and confused because of the unexpected and undesirable pregnancy. She states, "It was the worst thing that could happen to us then. I'd just begun working in a grocer's shop, just started earning money, and this happened. I didn't want the child, I didn't want Kalpana, I wanted her to die" (111). Mira is another character in the novel for whom motherhood is not an outcome of mutual desire. Mira's husband is obsessed with her and has proclivity towards physical intimacy rather than mental coordination. Trauma of forced sex destroys Mira's relationship with her husband. Being too young and dependent, she has no other alternative but to reticently surrender to her husband's bestiality. It generates an aversion towards life in her. She had been a vivacious child and her early poems suggest her enthusiasm towards life. She writes as a girl:

> Come, my brothers, come my sisters

> let us join our hands;
> a new road, a new way
> a new age begins. (4)

Her aim of becoming a poetess is shattered as soon as she ties nuptial knot. She fails to acclimatize herself in the new environment of loneliness and monotony. She is terrorised by her husband's obsession and starts hating herself for being a woman. She writes about her frightening experience:

> But tell me, friend, did Laxmi too
> Twist brocade tassels round her fingers
> and tremble, fearing the coming
> of the dark-clouded, engulfing night? (66)

While struggling with her emotional and psychological turmoil, Mira discovers her pregnancy. Urmi concludes, "He forced himself on her despite of it; it is out of this that Kishore was born" (83). Mira dies after giving birth to Kishore (Urmi's husband).

Kalpana, another female character of the novel, becomes a prey to her uncle Prabhakar's obsession. The novel has posited a very significant question of the necessity of marriage for a girl. Shakutai could get only misery and unwanted children out of her marriage, yet she wants her daughters to get married instead of giving them an opportunity to become independent and self-reliant. She attempts to suppress the incident of her daughter's rape, as she feels that it will be a stigma and minimize the chances of her marriage. Unable to understand such attitude, Dr. Bhaskar points out,

> Women are astonishing. I think it takes a hell of a lot of courage for a woman like that even to think of marriage. Have you seen her husband—Kalpana's father? No? I have. Well. . .' He lets out his breath in a laugh. A poor specimen. Vandana tells me he deserted this woman long back. What has she got out of marriage—except for the children, of course? And yet, she's longing for her daughter's marriage. (87)

Even Mira is unable to understand her mother's wish of getting her married when she herself has no stand in the family. Despite being a mother, she never takes any decisions regarding her children. She is more like a caretaker of the house with no right of decision-making—men are the decision-makers of the family. Mira recalls her mother's attitude, "Don't ask me," she used to say to us: "Nothing is in my hands" (126). Mira's married life has become a replica of her mother's life. She realizes that she too has lost her true self after marriage and is following the footsteps of her mother by playing the role of a suppressed and reticent partner. She writes,

> Whose face is this I see in the mirror,
> unsmiling grave, bedewed with fear?
> The daughter? No, Mother, I am now your shadow. (126)

As a feeble character with no authority over her own life, she evaluates her marital life as a distant spectator. Mira wants to question her mother for pushing her into the cul-de-sac of married life when she herself was made to bear its phantom throughout her life. She writes,

> I wish I could have asked her a question. 'Mother,' I always wanted to ask, 'Why do you want me to repeat your history when you despair of your own?' But she died and I will never know her answer now. (126)

Urmi's answer to the questions placed by Dr. Bhaskar and Mira echoes the traditional stand. She feels that women are keen to get their daughters married because they want to make them secure from other men. She states that marriage provides girls a security, "Security. You're safe from other men" (88). But through the character of Kalpana, Deshpande points out that women are not even safe in their own family. Kalpana is dishonoured by her own relative, i.e., uncle. It reflects that women should eschew their ideas of sneaking and ensconcing into the marital life in order to rescue themselves. In order to safeguard their honour, they have to stop considering their femininity as a weakness. They have to respect their womanliness and assert their existence as human beings in order to stop men from treating them as subordinates born to obey them. Vrinda Nabar points out in *Caste as*

Woman that the Indian girls are conditioned to shamefully hide any kind of sexual abuse they have to face, as it proves to be a stigma on their honour. She writes that the Indian girl

> is schooled into believing that her relationship with the male sex will have to be censored and shaped by her elders, i.e., that it ought not to develop in spontaneous or impulsive way. As a result, the question of discussing any experience of sexual harassment does not arise. An unpleasant encounter is usually suppressed, because these subjects are not open to frank discussion. Moreover, she is ashamed, even scared that she will be accused of having provoked the incident. (92)

Kalpana is also treated as a culprit for her own abuse. Shakutai considers Kalpana impertinent as she never pays attention to her warnings and cautions regarding men. Kalpana is not ready to submit to the patriarchal society and wants to live life on her own terms. After perceiving the stifling atmosphere around her, she concludes that economic independence can help her to overcome her deprived state and she works hard to achieve it. She despises the living conditions in which she has been brought up, and refuses to lead a docile and passive life like her mother. Kalpana wants to fulfil her dreams, but the sexual abuse and its associated social taboos smother her life. Shakutai blames Kalpana for being dishonoured:

> She's shamed us, we can never wipe off this blot. And Prakash blames me. What could I do? She was so self-willed. Cover yourself decently, I kept telling her, men are like animals. But she went her way. You should have seen her walking out, head in the air, caring for nobody. It's all her fault, Urmila, all her fault. (147)

Shakutai's concern for her daughter is evolved from the prevailing concepts of the society as stated by Vrinda Nabar. She does not like Kalpana's ideas regarding freedom and independence, as she knows that it will be difficult for them to resurge from the stigma. Disgraced women are never accepted by society. Hence Shakutai could not openly cry out against the injustice done to her daughter. Deshpande also exhibits that people perceive the physical outrage of a girl as a blot on the family. The policeman unconsciously displays this social cruelty when he says:

> We don't like rape cases, the man said. They're messy and troublesome, never straightforward. But forget that and think of the girl and her family. Do you think it'll do them any good to have it known the girl was raped? She's unmarried, people are bound to talk, her name would be smeared. For all you know she may be a professional, we see a lot of that. But if you ask me, the man said, she must have been out with a boyfriend—girls of that class always have boyfriends the families know nothing about it. Maybe after they had a bit of fun she was knocked down by a car. (88)

Kalpana is however not only a victim of the patriarchal society. Her aunt Sulu and mother Shakutai are also responsible for her pathetic state. Prabhakar's insensitive attitude towards Sulu due to her inability to produce a progeny reduces her to the status of a puppet. She reticently obeys all his demands and becomes a servile partner. Her life was full of fear—the fear of being rejected by Prabhakar and to live a life without a sheltering tree, i.e., a husband. She finds herself too feeble to cope with the outside world. The mere thought of surviving without a man in a men's world fills her with fear. Shakutai points out, "Sulu was frightened, she was always frightened because she had no children. She was afraid he would throw her out, take another wife" (192). Sulu always perceived Kalpana as her own daughter and is stunned when her husband proposes to marry Kalpana. Still she has no other option but to carry the marriage proposal to Shakutai. Sulu acquiesces to her husband's infidelity because she lacks her own independent individuality, and agrees to give Kalpana the status of a mistress in her own house. Deshpande speaks to Vanamala Viswanatha about the dependence syndrome in women:

> May be not being a working woman, I've been able to feel more for a housewife, who is most devalued . . . women who do not go out to work, who are literally trapped, who are scared, to get out of family relationships. Without that, she feels she has no claims whatever. Most women are still very emotionally dependent on the

> family—they want to be good daughters/wives/mothers always. A man wouldn't think so much about it. (235)

Sulu represents those childless Indian women to whom marriage and family is the only career. They completely efface their self-identity and transform themselves according to the desires of their husbands' families. The only purpose of their lives is to serve and satisfy their family members. In order to save their marriage from total collapse they sideline their own interests. Shakutai remembers that after marriage, Sulu's life was "full of fears" (195). Married women in India achieve a respectable position only when they bear children. Several sociological studies have been conducted about it. In one of the studies, Sudhir Kakar discusses how infertility makes a woman despicable. He has mentioned in *Women in Indian Society*:

> Subjectivity, in the world of feminine psychological experience, pregnancy is a deliverance from the insecurity, doubt and shame of infertility: 'Better be mud than a barren woman,' goes one proverb. Moreover, until very recently, in Hindu society,. as among the Jews, Muslims, and certain west African tribes, a childless wife could be repudiated (even if not divorced) by her husband who was permitted then to take another wife. (67)

Sulu's submissiveness works as a slow poison and gradually ends her sense of dignity and self-respect. Prabhakar's obsession makes him dishonour Kalpana and this incident works as a bombshell, blowing up her castle of endurance and patience. Unable to tolerate her husband's inhumane act, she commits suicide. Sulu becomes a prey to the age-old social convention which expounds that motherhood makes a woman complete. Contemplating on the condition of women in India, Urmi concludes that even after the declaration of many laws, much has to be achieved on the social level because the basic traits and norms of the society have remained unchanged. Women are still perceived as props and are used as tools to satiate the desires of men. Urmi concludes:

> It's never enough. It's like saying, "Look we have a woman Prime

> Minister; look how much our women have progressed; look how free they are. One Indira Gandhi in charge of the nation and a country full of women not allowed to take charge of their own lives. . . . No, Priti, laws can't change people's lives." (38)

The novel exposes the demeaning position of women in the society and the effect of gender discrimination on their psyche. The birth of a son is of paramount importance for the family as boys are considered as carriers of family name. Girls have to endure many humiliations. Vanaa, Kishore's step-sister, and Urmi's sister-in-law, strives hard to gain her father's attention and affection, but all her efforts are ignored as she is a girl. Her father is vainglorious to possess a son. Urmi recalls that "for him there was only Kishore" (52). Her father has no expectations from her because she simply does not exist for him. She points out, "Well! I'm lucky; my father expects nothing from me. In fact, I wonder whether he knows I exist" (53). Gender discrimination is greatly responsible for depriving women of equality with men on social level. Even our renowned law-givers have given preference to a son. Manu has stated:

> A man conquers the world by the birth of a son; he enjoys eternity by that of a grandson; and the great grandfather enjoys eternal happiness by the birth of a grandson's son. (Prabhu 242)

Vanaa, the modern, educated, economically independent woman, also wants to bear a son after giving birth to three daughters. Her psyche too is toned by centuries of conditioning which makes a woman feel complete only by giving birth to a son. Harish, Vanaa's husband, rebukes her for craving for a son. Though Vanaa is a career woman and is unable to handle her daughters properly, she cannot give up her hope of having a son. She confides in Urmi that Harish did not agree with her idea of giving birth to a third child in the hope of getting a son. Vanaa states that he "quoted population figures at me. And he said, one, surely I'm not the kind of woman who craves for sons, am I? And, two, what makes me think the next one will be a boy? He's right, only . . . I wouldn't have minded taking a chance" (81). Vanaa's situation also highlights the plight of working women in a society which suggests that the upbringing of the children is the duty and responsibility of the mother. The societal norms have proclaimed men as the masters of the house whose utmost duty is to provide bread and butter to their families. Women are relegated and confined to the domestic life in which men never participate. This traditional outlook is present even in the contemporary Indian society, stagnating the emancipation of women, weakening the roots of their progress, and suppressing their identity. "Mankind seemed to agree that children should be left under the management of women during their childhood" (Wollstonecraft 68). Vanaa finds it difficult to handle her job and domestic life together. Over and above her office duties, she has to attend to her family's demands too and feels unable to cope with the expounded work. She points out, "Urmi, why is it nobody thinks of blaming Harish? He's never around, but it is never his fault" (75). Urmi concludes: "Women take parenthood seriously; men not, not to the same extent, anyway" (76). Though men are excused from carrying out an active role in the domestic life, yet they have secured an unquestionable authority over their children. Most of the time, it is the father who takes decisions regarding his children. Women are expected to consent to it. Inni, another female character in the novel, is denied the right to make a decision regarding her children. Married at a young age, she is perplexed by the early motherhood to which she is subjected. As a young girl, she fails to look after her daughter Urmi. Later, she shares her feelings with her:

> 'I was frightened of you Urmi,' it bursts out of her. I was too young. I was not prepared to have a child. And you were not easy, you used to cry all the time, I didn't know how to soothe you. (199)

Urmi's father dislikes his wife's dependency on the servant to look after their daughter. He sends Urmi to his parental home to be brought up there. Inni's requests, pleas, tears and yearning cannot placate him to change his decision. She recalls, "Nothing could make him change his mind" (200). Forced to submit before his decision, she waits for years for her daughter to return to her. Inni represents those Indian mothers who are given no authority over their children. It is the father who dominates the children, whereas mother's authority is limited only upto their rearing and upbringing. Deshpande has exposed the complexity of human relationships in which women are treated like puppets. Imposed femininity and lack of assertiveness make them obey their spouses. The whole patriarchal system has diminished the status of women. The conditioning has toned them to limit their faculties and potential to the four walls of their domestic lives. To think otherwise fills them with guilt and shame. Urmi, the female protagonist, is the only female character in the novel, who is free from social conditioning. She maintains an independent stand and does not rely on her husband. As an educated and independent woman, she analyses the complexity of a woman's life and concludes that even the bitterness of life does not kill the desire to live—maybe Urmi wants to state that hope never dies. She points out:

> This is how life is for most of us, most of the time; we are absorbed in the daily routine of living. The main urge is always to survive. Mira realized that. Just as the utter futility of living overwhelms me, I am terrified by the thoughts of dying, of ceasing to be. (203)

The novel expounds the need to change the societal norms so that women can develop beyond the roles of wives, mothers, and daughters to which they are relegated. The novel also illustrates how emotional and psychological attachments with the family cause effacement of women's identity and self-respect. Yet the women characters of *The Binding Vine* never dream of living beyond the family life. They endure their traumas as a part of their existence and destiny. The only thing they desire is a pragmatic solution to their problems and hope for a better future with their families. Deshpande states in an interview to Uma Mahadevan-dasgupta: "But we always carry this dream of love, of being one with other humans, with another person. This is what makes life possible" (1).

The Binding Vine is a novel in which Deshpande has poignantly projected women trapped in the labyrinth of relationships. She has emphatically exposed various social diktats like motherhood, gender discrimination, servility of wives, and self-effacement, promoted by the patriarchal society for its benefit. The novel reflects Deshpande's mature vision subtly, depicting almost all the aspects related with the life of contemporary Indian women and laying bare their exploitation. The novel projects the Indian ethos in which women do not want a negation of family life—they want a drastic and sympathetic redefinition of the patterns of their married lives and attitudinal changes in the social perception of their roles.

A Matter of Time

The novels of Deshpande advocate the liberation of women from the bigoted social diktats prevailing unfortunately even in the contemporary Indian society. Freedom from dependence syndrome and acquisition of economic independence are considered by her as the major sources capable of imparting autonomy to women over their own lives, thoughts and actions, and thus restoring their true selves. Centuries of conditioning have enamelled their psyche to unquestioningly accept their existence as subordinates in a male-dominated society. Since childhood they are insinuated with the feminine traits which teach them to develop themselves for others and systematically erase their identity as individuals. The novel presents before us a female protagonist who is not ready to make any compromises at the cost of her self-respect to keep on clinging to her marital life which is clearly on the verge of total collapse. The novel concludes assertively with the feeling that today's women are finally becoming aware of their dignity and self-respect; and are not ready to endure the ignominy inflicted on them by the patriarchal society. They unhesitatingly want to establish themselves as autonomous beings, making decisions about themselves on their own.

Deshpande has deeply penetrated into the female psyche and realistically projected the tussle between modernity and conventional norms which rages continually in their mind, often generating a sense of guilt in them. In *A Matter of Time* the novelist portrays that women should overcome the subconscious feelings of guilt in order to assert their individuality and existence as human beings. She believes that the contemporary society inevitably needs a change in its dogmatic mindset. Elaborating the need to change, she writes in her essay "Literature and Morality":

> Human ideas of right and wrong do change from time to time, they often depend on the social, the cultural and the geographical context. What was wrong in one age is no longer so in another, what is wrong in one country or culture is right in another. In the *Gita*, for example, Krishna chides Arjuna for trying to apply the Dharma of an earlier age to his predicament [. . .]. Each age has its own dilemmas.

Deshpande's literature expounds that today's women should be gauged against the present social scenario and not against the conventional one. The traditional constricting modes of rearing up a girl child should be replaced by what is pertinent to them today as human beings. Women are traumatized when the conventional norms are imposed on them, killing their spontaneity. Doubts and questions in themselves are taken as signs of rebellion and are often brutally suppressed. Sumi, the female protagonist of *A Matter of Time*, refuses to submit before the social diktats which demand that women should not relegate themselves to the secondary position in the patriarchal society.

The story of *A Matter of Time* revolves around Sumi whose husband Gopal leaves her to live a life of ascetic solitude. Sumi returns to her parents' house and decides to take an independent stand and look after her daughters. She takes up the job of a school teacher and successfully shoulders the responsibility of a single parent till she meets an untimely death with her father in an accident. Her mother Kalyani, who is a traditional woman, braces herself to take up the responsibility of her granddaughters after mustering up enough strength to meet the challenges of life boldly. The novel embraces in it the story of three generations—grandmother, mother and daughters. The novel exhibits the conditions in which women have to survive and illustrates their effect on their way of perceiving and analysing the predicament of their lives which, despite the passage of decades, remains the same.

Kalyani, the mother of Sumi and Premi, leads a terrified childhood due to the atrocities of her mother, Manorama. As a child, she receives love only from her father, Vithalrao. Manorama is frustrated as she could not give birth to a son. Deshpande exposes preference given to sons in Indian families in many of her novels. *The Dark Holds No Terrors*, *If I Die Today* and *Roots and Shadows* describe the extent of gender discrimination experienced by girl-child within the family. Kalyani also faces the trauma of being a girl. Manorama becomes spasmodic in words and actions at the knowledge of her daughter receiving letters from an anonymous admirer. Kalyani's school education is stopped though her father wants her to become an engineer. She is hurriedly married to Manorama's brother Shripati without taking her consent and, "after this, Manorama felt secure. The property would remain in the family now. Her family" (129). Parallels can be drawn between Manorama and Saru's mother in *The Dark Holds No Terrors* as far as mother-daughter relationship is concerned. Saru's mother also exhibits hostility towards her daughter, but Saru manages to escape it, earning a medical degree and thereby establishing an independent stand. But Kalyani couldn't escape her mother's ruthlessness and reticently obeys all her decisions. After her marriage, she gives birth to two daughters, Sumi and Premi, but celebrations are allowed only when a son is born, though later he develops as a mentally-retarded boy. To Kalyani, happiness seems like a traveller making a brief sojourn in her life. The domination of her husband in her life has a traumatizing effect on her. Her pathetic state worsens when she loses her son accidentally at a railway station. Shripati accuses Kalyani for deliberately neglecting her son because she could not manage him. He squarely blames her, not so much by words but through his withdrawal. Shripati resembles other male characters in Deshpande's novels, particularly Urmi's father in *The Binding Vine*, who want to establish a dictatorial control and authority over their family members and do not tolerate any independent view. Kalyani is sent to her father's house where Manorama accuses her of bringing ill-fate to the family as her father dies soon after her arrival. Kalyani epitomizes traditional submissiveness and silence. She endures her mother's callousness and serves her during her illness. At her deathbed, Manorama calls for Shripati, which petrifies Kalyani:

> She stays awake at nights, terrified, walking out of fearful dreams when she did finally fall asleep, her body drenched in sweat. (153)

Shripati's dominance and dictatorship leave no space for companionship in his relationship with his wife. After he returns, they start living together. Since then, Kalyani has been spending her life by serving her husband, whereas Shripati takes her services for granted and never notices her existence. The communication gap between them never gives Kalyani an opportunity to defend herself against the accusations made by her husband. Kalyani laboriously works in her house and looks after her children and husband. She passively accepts the humiliations inflicted on her by Shripati. She is sidelined in his life and is reduced to the status of a slave in her own home. Simone de Beauvoir has sympathetically presented the isolated subjugation of housewives in *The Second* Sex:

> Thus woman's work within the home gives her no autonomy; it is not directly useful to society, it does not open out on the future, it produces nothing [. . .] far from being the matron, her occupation makes her dependent on her husband and children; she is justified through them; but in their lives she is only an inessential intermediary [. . .]. However respected she may be, she is subordinate, secondary, parasitic. The heavy curse that weighs upon her consists in this: the very meaning of her life is not in her hands. (175)

Kalyani too loses her self-respect in her marital life. She suffers mutely and gradually evolves a survival strategy by transferring her affection to her sister Goda, her two daughters and granddaughters. She represents those Indian women who cannot think beyond their marital life. They are conditioned to accept marriage as their career and trained to adjust and compromise even in the worst of humiliating situations. Deshpande's description of Kalyani brings it out clearly:

> They don't seem to realize that the real miracle is Kalyani herself, Kalyani who has survived intact in spite of what Shripati did to her. Kalyani who has survived Manorama's myriad acts of cruelty. (151)

Kalyani is never allowed by her mother to act according to her choice. Her upbringing gives her no opportunity to take her own decisions, rather it encourages her to develop those traits only which would help her in carrying out her domestic duties later in her marital life without any independent thinking. Mary Wollstonecraft penetratingly writes in *A Vindication of the Rights of Woman*:

> It is acknowledged that they spend many of the first years of their lives in acquiring a smattering of accomplishments; meanwhile strength of body and mind are sacrificed to libertine notions of beauty, to the desire of establishing themselves—the only way the women can rise in the world—by marriage. (10)

Kalyani too serves the family she finds herself in after her marriage. The socio-cultural patterns of the orthodox society have conditioned her and she has fatalistically internalized the idea of femininity. She is choiceless, predestined to accept what life holds out to her. While Kalyani presents a particular facet of women who meekly surrender before familial cruelty, her daughter Sumi presents another facet of contemporary Indian women who want to liberate themselves from the dependence syndrome. In the true sense Sumi is the protagonist of *A Matter of Time*, who fights all odds and ultimately asserts herself to gain independence. Sumi is portrayed as a modern, educated, middle-class woman. As a child, she has perceived the estranged relationship between her parents. Sumi does not want her children to watch her parents closely, when they come to live with them after her separation with Mohan. She wants to save them from the repercussions which most of the children usually face due to the frictions between their parents. Almost all the female protagonists of Deshpande have a strong urge to save their children from the agony which they have experienced in their childhood. Saru in *The Dark Holds No Terrors* faces gender discrimination as a child. Later in her life, she checks herself as a mother in order to protect her daughter from the humiliation which a girl child has to face because of the preference given to the male child in families. Sumi too wants to hide the growing friction with her husband Gopal from her daughters. Finally Gopal decides to live away from his family. Though Sumi never questions Gopal for escaping his responsibilities, yet she is desperate to know the reason for such strange decision. She contemplates:

> What is it Gopal, I will ask him, that makes a man in this age of acquisition and possession walk out of his family and all that he owns? Because, and I remember this so clearly, it was you who said that we are shaped by the age we live in, by the society we are part of.
>
> How then can you, in this age, a part of this society turn your back on everything in your life? Will you be able to give me an answer to this? (61)

Sumi's eldest daughter Aru often asks her to seek divorce from Gopal and advises her to meet a lawyer. She feels that her father should be made aware of his fault. Sumi rejects the idea because she knows that even if they sue Gopal and seek financial compensation, their family life will never become the same as it was earlier. For Sumi marriage is based on commitment and once broken, it can never be mended. She recalls his words:

> Marriage is not for everyone, the demand it makes, a lifetime of commitment—is not possible for all of us. (69)

Kalyani, a traditional woman, cannot bear the sight of her married daughter living outside the family domain without her husband. She desires reconciliation between Sumi and Gopal, yet

Sumi is determined not to compromise at the cost of her self-respect. Deshpande has projected the difference between the psychology of men and women, which has been created by the social conditioning. Women are made to feel guilty even for the slight deviation or neglect of the conventional norms, whereas men never feel ashamed of their follies. Gopal quits a long-standing marriage and decides to walk out because of ennui, yet never feels guilty for such irresponsible behaviour. He even fails in his aim of achieving asceticism. The sight of Sumi activates his dormant sensual desires which infuriate him. Gopal "is angry with himself, his very struggle against it making it difficult for him to subdue his body" (223). Gopal leaves his home because to him all relationships are spurious. The truth that he and Sudha, his sister, do not share common parents, as well as Sudha's lonely life after her operation, develop aversion in him towards human bonds. Sudha and Sumi prove to be stronger than Gopal. They face life in whatever form it comes before them. Gopal is only eager to grasp and view the negative aspects of relationships and everything appears yellow to his jaundiced eyes. Gopal has been portrayed as a confused person whose background is partially responsible for such behaviour. Absence of any attempt for filling up the familial void on his part, and also of any attachment for children he has left in lurch, epitomize the confusion of an age in which the priorities have been muddled up.

Sumi continues her life and unleashes her psyche from the dogma of possessing a sheltering tree, i.e., a husband. She has an independent mind with the power of analysing and implementing her thoughts. She also possesses a maturity not to overreact. Sumi's daughter Charu is hopeful that one day her father would return and everything will become normal. She asks Sumi whether she will accept Gopal and forgive his faults. Sumi has assessed the situation in a more practical manner, and responds accordingly:

> High and mighty? No, I can never be that. But taking him back. I don't know, Charu that sounds odd to me. As if he's a pet dog who's strayed away or something. No Charu, I am not a good

> hater. I can never keep it up for long. But even if he comes back, things can never be the way they are, you know that, don't you? (194)

Sumi does not lament her lonely state. Her only wish to buy a house for her daughters can not materialize due to her limited income. Sudha's son Ramesh extends his financial help to Sumi, which according to him is her right and not a charity done to her. Sumi again rationally analyses her position:

> You know Ramesh, I've begun to think that what Gopal has really done is to take sanyas. I'm surprised none of you have thought of that. But look what's happened. It's not he who is going around with the begging bowl, it's I who am doing it. (123)

Sumi's words present before us the plight of middle-class Indian women—the plight of women due to their dependence on men. Deshpande has presented the pathetic state of women due to their feminine traits which teach them to ensconce in their family. While doing so, they inculcate self-denial and self-abnegation in order to satiate the desires of their family members. In this process, they lose their self-identity and make themselves dependent on other throughout their life. Sumi refuses to be relegated to this state of dependence and realizes the potential of her dormant strength only when her husband deserts her. Almost all the female protagonists of Deshpande are financially independent or desire so. She feels that economically sufficed women can liberate themselves from feminine traits of submissiveness and servility as they learn to take decisions on their own. Sumi takes up the job of a school teacher and supports her family. Her economic independence gives her strength to carry on her responsibilities towards her family. She learns not to remain dependent on anyone. She also leaves her husband very much alone—neither questioning his devotion to her children, nor insisting on his fulfilling such filial duties. She simply accepts it as a fate of life. Critics have often questioned this attitude. However a true analysis of her character tells us that her acceptance is a sign of strength and not of weakness—she does not seek pity, does not even want her rights if she has to petition before a person—even though the person has been her husband. Deshpande in her interview to Vimala Rama Rao has highlighted Sumi's inner strength:

> Sumi's acceptance is not passive. She blocks out the unpleasantness. She has a good opinion of herself, she is more concerned with getting on with life. She does not want pity, she would do anything for pride. She distances even her husband. The point is, they are both unusual. People are puzzled by the abandoned wife not feeling bad. (256)

Society expects a woman to live a lamenting life if she is abandoned by her husband or becomes a widow. Deshpande has consistently opposed this view in her fiction. Her story "A Man and a Woman" also describes a widow being criticized by her relatives for active participation in life. Possession of a husband is considered as the only desire and aim of a woman's life, without which they are expected to eschew all their happiness and desires. But Sumi is a confident and courageous woman who decides to face the challenges of life alone. She does not think of getting back to her marital life and live a subjugated life without a purpose. Deshpande believes that women have to assert their true selves and go beyond the centuries of conditioning. Sumi is a fictional representative of this idea which has been vociferously advocated by feminists. Betty Friedan has also suggested that women should overcome their femininity in order to establish their individuality. She states in *The Feminine Mystique*, "Now that education, freedom, the right to work on the great human frontiers—all the roads by which men have realised themselves—are open to women, only the shadow of the past enshrined in the mystique of feminine fulfilment keeps women from finding their road" (326). Sumi is able to transcend the hold of feminine traits on her psyche instead of dragging a relationship which has already collapsed. She appears before us as a modern woman who has the reasoning power and solves her problems pragmatically.

Aru, the eldest daughter of Sumi, is a young girl of seventeen who achieves maturity at quite an early age owing to her family circumstances. After her father's desertion, she finds her family in a dilapidated condition. Aru and her sister Charu represent the predicament of those children who have to bear the pitiful glances of people eager to label them as fatherless children. Aru develops revulsion for her father and in his absence looks after her family. Sumi analyses her daughter's behaviour. She

> feels that Aru wants to be the man of the family. She wants to take Gopal's place, she wants to fill the blank Gopal has left in their lives. Aru is trying to steer up her mother and sister through the stormy passage of change. In this however, she comes up against Kalyani. Aru finds Kalyani's restrictions as heart-burning and hard to bear. (36)

Aru has to bear the brunt of her parents' separation. Her father's desertion, her grandfather's strange and rude behaviour towards her grandmother and Goda's complaints that men have established monopoly over women reducing them to the status of puppets inculcate in her a revulsion for men. The silence maintained by Kalyani is inexplicable to her. She wants Kalyani to define her position in the house whereas Charu, her sister, feels that it is impossible to question Shripati for he is the man of authority. Aru also finds it strange that though Shripati has accepted Kalyani's services, yet has not talked to her since the past thirty years of their marital life. Aru concludes that Kalyani's servility and submission have reduced her to a pathetic state. She comments:

> It is important to her that you speak out, state the truth that you stand up and defend yourself, that you refuse to be misjudged. (143)

The novel highlights the plight of children in broken marriages. Aru feels that elders sometime make wild decisions in their lives without contemplating on their repercussions. It leads to a chaotic mismanagement not only of their lives, but also of the lives of those who are related with them. Aru perceives Gopal as a person who has deprived them of all the happiness of their life. He has snatched from them a happy family life and a respectable place in society and therefore she is not ready to let him go scot-free. In her belligerent state, she considers him as a callous husband. Her advocate friend Surekha tries her best to bring reconciliation between Aru's parents, but all her attempts prove futile. Aru finally learns that nothing can be done to bridge the gap between her parents. Aru comes across as a sensitive youngster, unable to overcome the trauma of her parents' separation. She is presented as a foil to her younger sister Charu who has a pragmatic approach towards life and does not want to be a victim of circumstances. She expounds, "They can't mess up my life. I'm going on with what I want to do" (58). Charu decides to join a medical college for which she is not hesitant to seek financial help from Sumi's sister Premi-mavshi.

A Matter of Time exhibits and records the changes occurring in women's perception of life. From Kalyani to Aru there appears a drastic change in thinking, action, reasoning and analysing the apprehensions of women's life. Deshpande states about Aru in her interview to Vimala Rama Rao:

> The sense of family history, the context in which Aru tries to make out her own identity is important. Aru is an observer, to me she is the focal point. It is through her parents' story that she reaches her grandparents' story. Two different generations standing on the same ground—that is very important to me. Aru is angry with her mother. She sees Kalyani not as a victim but as a woman come out of all that victimisation intact, like the end of a story. (257)

The novel compels the reader to review the established social dogmas which confine women within the four walls of family and treat them with contemptuous inferiority. Ideally marriage is considered as a sacred union of man and woman leading to the evolution of family. But the domineering status of men changes it into a macabre struggle for women who feel threatened by the importuning attitude of their male counterparts. Children feel insecure after watching the fragile relations. Aru too feels that they are trapped by the greatest fear:

> The fear of losing face. Gopal's desertion is not just a tragedy, it's

> both a shame and a disgrace. There was a time when a man could have walked out of his home and the seamless whole of the joint family would have enclosed his wife and children, covered his absence. Now the rent in the fabric gaping wide is there for all to see. (137)

The servile docility remains unnoticed as men take it for granted. Shripati never acknowledges Kalyani's presence and even in his will addresses her not as his wife but as the daughter of Vithalrao and Manoramabai. Kalyani and Sumi have to face their husband's indifference, but their attitudes are different. Kalyani, as a traditional woman, is the epitome of silence and patience, whereas Sumi, as a modern woman, exhibits a change in psychology by not submitting her pride and dignity to Gopal. She dies with Shripati in an accident just when she was on the brink of starting a new life with her own efforts. Deshpande states about the unhappy conclusion in an interview to Vimala Rama Rao:

> So was I unhappy over Sumi's death, but it just happened; it was not deliberate. Sumi without a husband, the economic part would be most important. Money is very important to me like Jane Austen. (257)

Deshpande also asserts Sumi's death does not imply her defeat. She states in her essay "Literature and Morality":

> In my novel *A Matter of Time* for example, a character Sumi dies at a point close to the end. There was a lot of criticism about this. Since Sumi, a woman who had been deserted by her husband, was just learning to cope, to crave out a new life for herself, since she was on the brink of shaping an independent existence for herself, the idea was that her death was a betrayal of what was right, the cause of feminism, which was assumed to be my purpose. I should have let my character who was growing out of victimhood into an independent human being, alive. I should have let her go to the logical end of her growth. I have to admit that I was surprised myself at her death. I would have liked her to live. I admired the way she had grown as a human being. But the remorseless logic of the story, of the voice that was dictating the story, told me that she had

> to die. Her struggle to learn the truth of her condition as a human being was what mattered [. . .]. The death of a good character is not a defeat for morality.

Sumi's death does not project the end of the hope of women's resurrection from their pathetic state. The suppressed Kalyani gathers all her courage and strength and takes hold of her grand-daughters' lives. Kalyani too begins to talk about life. She admonishes Aru for her growing hatred for men. She states, "You can't stop living because someone else has got hurt. . . . Coming from a woman who never speaks of 'life,' the statement cannot be ignored, it has to be taken note of. Aru recognizes this" (198). She too gradually learns to speak of her hidden emotions, which she has been suppressing since years. Shripati's will, which mentions her as the daughter of Manoramabai and Vithalrao, strengthens her as she feels that it has restored her lost identity. The death of Shripati and Sumi brings a drastic change in her personality. She acts decisively and makes Gopal realize that he has forfeited his place in their lives. He moves forward to console his daughters, but finds Kalyani available for them at the time of despair.

Deshpande's novels project the Indian ethics—as her women characters are purely Indian. With the advent of modernization, we find a clash between modernism and established norms. Indian women have finally recognized their strength and are gradually rejecting the constricting conventional norms. Deshpande's novels reveal that this change is inevitable. But in her works, this change is neither sudden nor violent. It's a result of one's growing and constant realization of independent identity, nurturing and promoting a firmer grasp over one's surroundings. This change is reflected in *A Matter of Time* also. The changing psychology of women is breaking down the age-old barriers. A gradual development in women's personality from reticent, naive partner to self-realization and independence is visible.

Deshpande advocates total independence for women—an independence which should pervade their thoughts, expressions and actions. Relationships define womanhood and it is within this frame that the whole network of their world has been woven. Deshpande's female protagonists do not want to transcend or negate these bonds, they want their existence to be identified and respected by their male counterparts. *A Matter of Time* assertively speaks about the independence of women and the acknowledgement of their rights. It also depicts that the man-woman relationship can be restored to the axis of equal dignity only through the dilution of ego and mutual understanding of each other's needs.

Small Remedies

Shashi Deshpande's work encompasses a wide range of women characters. All of them try to acclimatize themselves to the social and marital upheavals which they experience due to the presence of modern as well as conventional traits in the contemporary Indian society. Her novels deal subtly with various social, marital and professional problems faced by women and their intense desire to overcome them. Her women reflect an optimistic attitude towards life and have a desire to actively participate in it. Madhu, the female protagonist of *Small Remedies*, is no exception to it. She is able to transcend the tragic loss and experiences of her life and develop a spontaneous surge towards it, searching for some permanent values amidst her chaotic life. The novelist projects that women should realize that there are small remedies in terms of love, care, affection and memories; which, if considered, can help them to overcome the haunting grief associated with memories. Madhu understands and internalizes this reality of life through a variety of experiences. She learns that mishaps can never be ameliorated and loss can never be amended, but it is the warmth of relationships which expounds that the loss is never a total loss. *Small Remedies*, besides acting as a lodestar for women who are suffering from the maelstrom of emotions due to traumas and tragic losses, also depicts women exposed to various social pressures in their lives.

The story of *Small Remedies* unfolds gradually on the basis of the events of four female characters—Madhu, Leela, Savitribai Indorekar and Hasina. These women have to overcome the challenges and complexities associated with their individual family and social life. Deshpande has illustrated Madhu as a doting mother and wife, Leela and Savitribai Indorekar as assertive and independent women and Hasina as a woman desirous of realizing her latent abilities and attaining the heights of perfection. All these women have the strength to solve the labyrinth of their lives and transmute their thoughts and desires into reality. These women foray into the male chauvinistic world to establish their autonomy. Deshpande's women refuse to be acquiescent, suffering and sacrificing lot. They are women who are conscious of their emotional needs and hence cry for a change of order that starves them of individual fulfilment. They are women who long for an atmosphere congenial for self-expression and conducive to self-fulfilment. To understand them in a better way, it is required to analyse them individually.

Madhu is the protagonist, as well as the narrator of *Small Remedies*. She is a motherless child brought up by her father who is a doctor by profession at Neemgaon. After her father's death, she is brought up in her aunt's family. Her experiences with her incompatible cousin Paula are described in detail to give us a glimpse of her formative years. She feels lonely and perplexed which makes her extremely sensitive despite the encouragement provided by Leela and Joe. Her marriage with Som and the birth of a son subside her trauma. Madhu had never experienced the warmth of motherly affection and never really bothered to possess a motherly figure in her life. She summarizes mothers as, "drab creatures, forever working, scolding their children; certainly they are not the women to arouse a sense of deprivation in me" (182). But she finds a great transformation in her personality after the attainment of motherhood and states: "Mother love is one of the great wonders of this world" (184). The death of her son Adit in the communal riots at the time of demolition of Babri Masjid disturbs her mental balance as she hunts for her dead son in public places and streets. Death of Adit tears her apart. She concludes, "Death is not an event, it's an end. It's like a nuclear devastation; there's nothing left. Som and I are moving through the rubble of our devastated lives, searching for something, for any bits and pieces of our past. But there's nothing" (211). Madhu holds herself responsible for the death of her son Adit. It was the estrangement in her relationship with Som which made Adit leave home suddenly and become a prey to the riots occurring in the city. In order to recover from her disturbed mental state and sense of guilt, Madhu decides to leave Som for sometime and goes to Bhavanipur where she tries to occupy herself in writing a biography of Savitribai Indorekar, a great classical singer of her time.

Almost all the novels of Deshpande trace the girlhood and wifehood of their female protagonists. These two phases of Madhu's life too are poignantly projected by the novelist. Compared to the childhood of other female protagonists of Deshpande's novels, Madhu's childhood seems to be the happiest of all. Her childhood at the parental home is free from the trauma of gender discrimination and social conditioning. Madhu, though a motherless child, neither feels insecure, nor longs for her mother's existence because her father's love and affection never make her feel lonely. Madhu recalls their intimacy:

> We were always comfortable and easy with one another. The space between us was not crowded with demands, doubts, assertions, or questions. There was enough air for us to breathe easily. Ours was a relationship built, not on information, but on trust. (175)

She gets acquainted with the female world through Babu, the servant appointed to look after her. Madhu recalls that Babu taught her "about being a girl" by cautioning her often, "Don't run out in your petticoat," or "You must come home before dark," or "If those boys talk to you, ignore them" (101-2). When she grew up "officially" a maid was appointed to wash her clothes and follow her when she was home. She dislikes the presence of the old woman but never complains to her father because she feels that "Babu's word, in many matters, is the final law" (102). It is through Babu that she learns a little bit about femininity. She is made aware of her existence as a female, yet it is not revealed cruelly. She spends a happy childhood, free from social conditioning. However, after her father's death, she has some bitter experiences at Leela's home. She fails to acclimatize to the strange, new surroundings, and recalls:

> I enter their home [. . .], but I never become part of the family. This is not a proper family, nor the kind of family the girls evoked in their 'house house' game, either. Joe and Leela are a couple, but they are not father and mother. Paula draws a line around Joe and herself, she ignores Leela completely [. . .].
>
> I can never be a part of this set-up, I have no place in it, not even as an outsider. (102)

Madhu could clearly perceive the springing hatred of Paula for her, who despises her presence in the family. Madhu hears her "strings of abuses" (119) like "a beggar, a disgusting pauper, a savage, a stinking bit of filth" (119). Madhu started "to dread at night" (119) and Paula appears to her as a "monster" (119) whose appearance freezes her "into immobility" (118-19). Madhu endures the torturous attitude of Paula silently. Her sojourn at Leela's house acquaints her with the harsh realities of life. Though lot of love was showered on her by Joe and Leela, she was aware of her own position in the house as an alien and orphan who was brought to their house and provided with shelter and security. She feels obliged and points out:

> But making myself invisible, merging into the background, had become second nature to me after my father's death. Living, even for that brief while, in Joe's house, I became a very circumspect girl, not letting any part of my life spill over into Leela and Joe's life, into that house. Paula's hatred and fury reminded me each moment that I was an intruder. I knew I had to stay out of sight, I had to remain unnoticed, not for myself alone, but for Leela's sake as well. (160)

Madhu despises her dependence on Joe and therefore decides to leave her studies and starts working. Though Leela and Joe wanted her to go for higher studies, she was "determined" (83) to earn and "become independent" (83) because the money left by her father had finished. She rejects the financial help offered by Joe as she wanted to overcome her state of being a parasite. Madhu appears as a girl who wants to maintain her dignity and self-respect and refuses to stick to the dependence syndrome as evident in the society. Madhu neither wanted to lead a burdened and obliged life, nor wanted to accept any charity. She appears as a courageous girl who is not ready to reconcile to the challenges of her life by accepting them as her ill-fate, and emerges as a woman with strength and vivacity to become successful in life with her own efforts. She does not burden her relations with the responsibility of her life. She scoops out the cherished feminine traits which encourage a girl to lead a dependent life on her guardians till she is married. The novels of Deshpande speak volumes about the economic independence of women. In almost all her novels, she has presented working women—Saru as a doctor in *The Dark Holds No Terrors*, Manju as a teacher in *If I Die Today*, Kshama, the headmistress in *Come Up and Be Dead*, Indu, a writer in *Roots and Shadows*, Urmila, a teacher in *The Binding Vine*, and Sumi as a teacher in *A Matter of Time*. Though their economic independence does not provide complete autonomy to them and they are still insulted and treated shabbily by their husbands, yet it definitely enables them to think independently and make decisions which help them to solve the complexities of their marital life. Madhu too gets a job at Hamid Merchant's 'City View' and establishes her independent stand.

Deshpande has also projected the problems of working women. She points out that working women are overburdened by the responsibilities of job and family. Vanaa in *The Binding Vine* becomes perplexed when she has to fulfil her familial responsibilities along with her job and gets no help from her husband. The novelist has also discussed the ugly fact of sexual harassment of working women by their male colleagues. Madhu endures the lusty eyes of her senior Dalvi. He accuses her of occupying the position because she was Joe's niece. Madhu describes:

> He works out his hostility in other ways too. He comes to my table to berate me, his face angry, his tone sarcastic, but his eyes and his hands say other things. The eyes dart over my face, drop down to my body, they linger over my breasts, his hands brush lightly, and seemingly by accident, but I know with deliberate intent, against my body, my face. When he comes close to me, in what seems like intense anger, the short distance between us crackles with his desires, his lust. (84-85)

Women are exploited sexually once they move out to establish their independent stand. They reticently tolerate the humiliations inflicted upon them by their male associates because any kind of retaliation will become a permanent stigma on them. Madhu too pays no heed to Dalvi's lust prone actions as she knows that people look with suspicion at her relationship with Dalvi. She states, "Dalvi's role in my life is talked about, commented on" (86). The novel reveals the true picture of the chauvinistic society which chastises even those women who are the victims of sexual harassment and exploitation.

Deshpande has also depicted the complexity in husband-wife relationship in which women efface their true self in order to satisfy their male counterparts. She has projected that different moral codes have been established for men and women. Infidelity by women is considered as a sacrilege whereas men are never made to feel guilty. Simone de Beauvoir points out in *The Second Sex*:

> woman is not concerned to establish individual relations with a chosen mate, but to carry on the feminine functions in their generality, [. . .]. In regard to her erotic fate, two essential consequences follow: first, she has no right to any sexual activity apart from marriage; sexual intercourse thus becoming an institution, desire and gratification to the interest of society for both sexes; but man, being transcended towards the universal worker and citizen, can en-

> joy contingent pleasures before marriage and extra-maritally. (156-57)

Small Remedies portrays the estrangement in husband-wife relationship due to the momentary infidelity, unconsciously committed by the wife. Madhu reveals to Som a secret which was buried in the innermost recesses of her mind. When she was a girl of fifteen, she had once slept with a man who had later committed suicide. Madhu recalls that the thought of her father's death had made her hysterical. A man approaches her to pacify her and while doing so they indulge in physical gratification. Her sense of insecurity and loneliness is erased by the presence of the man. She recalls, "I want it back, the closeness, the comfort that the closeness brought me. His body seems to be the one centre in my disintegrating world, the one solid thing I can hold on to in the maelstrom whirling about me" (267-68). Som had admired Madhu for her "height," "dignity," "simplicity" and found her as delicate as a "glass" (229). Her revelation of her momentary intimacy with a man in her childhood, and total absence of guilt which the society associates with it, serve as a catastrophe in their relationship. Madhu points out:

> But it's the single act of sex that Som holds on to, it's this fact that he can't let go of, as if it's been welded into his palm. Purity, chastity, an intact hymen—these are the things Som is thinking of, these are the truths that matter? (262)

He asks her to tell everything about her past and reveal all the hidden relationships she may have had in her past and "bringing up the names of all those he imagines could have been" (256) her lovers. Som becomes "savage in his love-making" (257). The problem of sadism within marriage is sensitively treated by Deshpande in *The Dark Holds No Terrors* and *The Binding Vine* also. Madhu reticently endures the sadistic attitude of her husband. Gradually he stops having any kind of physical intimacy with her. Madhu realizes that nothing could sort out the estrangement in their relationship because, "trust has gone. Without trust there can be no truth, without it our relationship has no chance of survival. Nothing can survive without trust" (259). Her efforts to affect a compromise between them prove futile and differences remain unsettled. Emotionally disturbed by the tragic death of her son and the estrangement with her husband, she decides to move away from her depressed surroundings and goes to Bhavanipur where she had to write a biography of Savitribai Indorekar. Her stay at Bhavanipur with Hari and Lata teaches her that one should be open and receptive to life. Madhu realizes that the spontaneity of life arrives only with a cessation of planning and openness to change. She understands that the more one desires to manage life according to some preconceived pattern, the more irritated, frustrated and fearful one becomes. Her constant anxiety is replaced by appreciative confidence and a desire to reassess her life in the context of its different relationships. Madhu's attempt to write a biography of the vocalist Savitribai Indorekar proves to be an internal voyage, resulting in her glorious surrender before the force of truth. While watching the 'Upanayan' of a boy in a temple, Madhu discovers that his mother was a widow. As Madhu saw the woman receding, she contemplates:

> I watch her retreating back and think; so many of us walking this earth with our pain, our sorrow concealed within ourselves, so many of us hiding our suffering, going about as if all is well, so many of us surviving our loss, our grief. It's a miracle, nothing less than a miracle. (315)

It is this thought which pacifies her agony. She finishes her interview with Savitribai and after attending the live performance of Hasina decides to go back to Som. She also realizes that her miseries are caused by misconceptions and distorted egotistic perspectives, and the ultimate solution to these must emerge from within her own self. She readies herself to face the realities of life boldly. She understands that as a human being one cannot escape from the mishaps and miseries of life. She had avoided talking to her husband about their son's death, but now decides to go back to him to mourn together for their son at his death anniversary. She understands that though Adit's death has destroyed the possibility of any dreams for them, yet life has to be lived and continued. She states, "Now I am beginning to understand. It's not just living children who need to be free, the dead clamour for release as well" (323). She realizes that it is the memory which makes us live with those who are dead. She states that as "long as there is memory, there's always the possibility of retrieval, as long as there is memory, loss is never total" (324).

Deshpande has depicted various facets of motherhood boldly in her novels. The novelist does not believe in portraying only the stereotyped image of mothers, because she feels that every woman has her own way of dealing with roles and relationships and must therefore have her individual way of treating and tackling them. Thus she has depicted nonchalant attitude of mothers (like Saru's mother in *The Dark Holds No Terrors*) towards their daughters and also women (like Manju in *If I Die Today*) who treat motherhood as a role which limits a woman's freedom. She has also portrayed doting mothers like Urmila in *The Binding Vine*, Sumi in *A Matter of Time* and Madhu in *Small Remedies*. Madhu is the only female protagonist of Deshpande who has been portrayed as the cooing, sacrificing and sentimental mother. Adit was born after two years of marital life. Her child established another link with Som, i.e., of being parents of Adit—"Aditya-che Baba" and "Aditya-Chi Aai" (229). She leaves her job as soon as she becomes pregnant because she wants to give her child not "a measured amount of time" (146) but her whole attention. She becomes confined to her motherhood and concludes, "Motherhood absorbs all of me, I've nothing left for anyone, for anything" (146). A motherless child herself, Madhu feels immense pleasure and pride after becoming a mother. She takes great care while looking after her son. She is unable to gauge her feelings when she sees the child and the sight of the baby makes her feel "privileged, enjoying something rare" (89). She realizes that all her aspirations, hopes and wishes have been fulfilled and she is left with no other desire to achieve. She states, "What can you give me, my Lord, I, who have everything?" (89) Whenever Adit shows any symptom of ailment, she immediately rings the pediatrician, Rajani. She wants to guard and protect her son from any kind of pain or misery. She contemplates on the drastic change in her life and personality after attaining motherhood:

> Motherhood takes over my life, it makes me over into an entirely different person. The in-control-of-herself Madhu is lost, gone forever. It's my baby's dependence that changes me; my place in this universe is marked out now. (183)

Madhu is the only protagonist of Deshpande who so immensely glorifies her status as a mother. Her motherhood was a conscious and willing decision, an outcome of mutual understanding—it was not imposed on her.

Small Remedies also presents defiant females through Leela, Savitribai Indorekar and Hasina. Leela appears as an enfant terrible who smashes all the established norms set by the society for women. Joe fell in love with Leela who was "living in the crowded chawls among the cotton mills" (99). It was TB Bacillus which motivated Leela to send women suffering from the disease to Joe who had established a clinic for such patients. She was a widow who used to wear cotton saris manufactured at the mill where her husband used to work before he died. Madhu describes about Joe and Leela:

> Joe was an ardent lover, he waited fifteen years to marry Leela, he waited patiently until she agreed to marry him. Joe married Leela in spite of Paula [. . .]. And yet Joe, who could never displease Paula, married Leela. Her own family, her husband Vasant's family that is, were all for it. It was Paula and her feelings that kept Leela from giving into Joe's importunities. She gave in finally because—she told me herself—she didn't think it was right to deprive Joe and herself of happiness 'because of a spoilt brat.' (180)

Both Leela and Madhu's mother Kaveri were labelled as "rebels of the family" (45). Leela was cast as a "figure little girls were threatened with when they were disobedient or troublesome" (45). She was treated as a "black sheep" (45) because being a widow she had remarried, and that too with a Christian. This response in itself highlights the discrimination against women and the tendency to judge their merit on the basis of their marriage. Madhu points out:

> Leela's other activities did not matter to them, none of her achievements registered. Her years of teaching, her role in the trade unions, her work among the factory workers—these were blanked out, they did not exist. (46)

Deshpande depicts that a woman is not judged by her professional/academic achievements but by her marital position. Women are appreciated only when they follow the feminine traits established by the patriarchal society. The novelist has taken up the issue of widow remarriage in some of her stories also—"Rain," "A Man and a Woman" and "Cruelty Game." Through these stories, she has expounded that the widows should be given a chance to live their lives according to their desire. In the contemporary Indian society, the widows are made to accept their lives as despicable and are forced to lead an ascetic life. But Leela was not ready to surrender. Her father approached her "to take her back home after Vasant's death." At home she could have lived a "life of reasonable comfort" (234). But she decides to look after her in-laws as they needed her help and support. She decides to live with them because:

> there was Mai, there were her two brothers-in-law; they were her family now. She had to help them, to earn a living for all of them until the boys were educated. She refused to go back home, perhaps she said things which caused a rift. There was no communication with her family after that. The next time Leela went home was nearly thirty years later. (234)

Leela also refuses to accept the restrictions imposed on widows and marries Joe against the wishes of her guardians. She is capable of taking her own decisions and is not guided by others. As she herself has led an independent life, she understands the strong urge in Madhu to free herself from the dependence syndrome as soon as possible in her life.

Savitribai Indorekar is another female character in the novel who dares to go beyond the demarcations set for women by an orthodox society. Her interest in music forces her to approach her father-in-law and tell him about it. He understands her desire to learn music and appoints a lady music teacher who comes with a tabla-master, Ghulam Ahmed. However, Savitribai was not satisfied with her home tuitions and wished to learn music from a great maestro. She was aware that her conventional family would never allow her to fulfil her desire. Savitribai becomes an ardent fan of Guruji after hearing his performance and flees with Ghulam Saab to meet him. Madhu recalls Bai's relationship with Guruji which was "already a legend" (127). She states:

> There is no music lover, no Savitribai admirer, who hasn't heard the story of her search for a teacher. Her determination, after she heard Pundit Kashinath Buwa, that he had to be the one. Her persistence in seeking him out, the long wait before he finally agreed to take her on as a pupil. These are all the much-told, much dramatized incidents of her life. (127)

After understanding her earnest desire to learn music, Punditji finally accepts her as his disciple. While living with Ghulam Ahmed, she gives birth to Meenakshi. Her daughter has to endure the cruelty of other children who tease her for being the child of a Muslim father and a Hindu mother. Meenakshi despises the presence of Ghulam Saab in her life and never accepts him as her father. She concocts a story to tell her chiding friends that her father is an advocate and lives in Pune. Savitribai totally ignores her daughter's trauma, pain and loneliness. She devotes her time to practise music in order to achieve perfection. Talking to Madhu, she reminisces about her learning years:

> They were the best years of my life, she says to me, 'Life was simple. Just one room to live in, nothing to think or worry about except my class with Guruji. The days I didn't go for my class, I spent in absorbing what he had taught me, I did my riaz for nearly ten to twelve hours a day, can you believe it!' (133)

Madhu, who had been a neighbour of Savitribai in her childhood, is shocked to see that she has completely erased the presence of her daughter from her life:

> I've been looking at the fact of Bai's silence about Munni, turning it around, seeing sometimes a disease-induced amnesia, at other times a deliberate cruel forgetting. But perhaps it's neither, maybe it's just indifference that has made forgetting possible. Indifference is, after all, the best armour you can wear.
>
> If I don't care, I can't be hurt. (107)

Madhu who herself has been a loving mother, cannot understand Savitribai's negligent attitude towards her daughter. She also realizes that the great classical singer has omitted the name of Ghulam Saab from her description of her journey of becoming a classical singer. This was deliberately done in order to attain a positive image in a conformist society, which always measures a woman not by her achievements, but by her chastity. It was this fear of being devoid of respectability in the society that Savitribai Indorekar hides the existence of her daughter whom she had given her maiden name—Meenakshi Indorekar. "Making her out as her child alone, not the child of her marriage, not the child of her lover" (149). Madhu finds Bai's narration of her past incomplete and partial, "In this story I see the artist, the woman in search of her genius, of her destiny. But the artist was born of the woman" (133).

Though Savitribai Indorekar has the grit to transgress the barriers of her conventional family life in order to transmute her thoughts of becoming a great classical singer into reality, she still is unwilling to acknowledge the presence of a daughter born out of wedlock, as it could have jeopardized her efforts to become a great singer and tarnish her public image. She knows that the existence of her daughter can raise many questions regarding her respectability and therefore decides to obliterate her from her life. It reveals the true picture of the patriarchal society which wants to limit a woman to the four walls of family life. Women are not encouraged to think about the implementation of their dreams and ambitions. If Bai's family had been supportive of her, she could have fulfilled her responsibilities towards home and simultaneously lead a professional life. Savitribai succeeds in her professional life but fails in her family life because of the pressures of a patriarchal society which treats women as possessions and not as companions. Through the character of Savitribai, Deshpande seems to subtly suggest that the prevailing value system of India should come in for a radical revision and the social institutions and other props of civilization should be thoroughly reengineered to make life more agreeable for women.

Hasina, the grand-daughter of Ghulam Saab, is another facet of women fighting to establish their identity. Madhu knows her as "Bai's student, as well as her companion" (59). When Bai gets a stroke, Madhu gets a chance to become intimate with her. Madhu comes to know that she is the grand-daughter of Ghulam Saab. She considers Savitribai as a "great musician" (272) and Ghulam Saab as the best tabla player of his time. But Hasina couldn't guess the reason of their separation. She was only aware that he finally "returned home, to the family he had deserted" (274). By the time he returned his daughters were married and sons had "their own families" (274). Ghulam Saab's wife disliked his "vegetarianism" (274) as it "linked him to that woman, his mistress" (274). His wife had changed drastically into a waspish woman because of leading "the life of an abandoned wife, of living on the charity of others, of bringing up children on her own, had embittered her" (274). Hasina always watched her grand-father when he taught the children. Nobody noticed her presence till the day she pressed the key of the harmonium as asked by Ghulam Saab. She insisted on learning tabla but he rejected the idea saying that, "Women can't play tabla" (275). Instead he taught her "vocal music" (275). In spite of her mother and grandmother's objections, Hasina was taught music at Bombay by an "old colleague" (276) of her grandfather. Finally he tells her about his relationship with Bai and together they listen to her records and cassettes (276). Hasina gets an opportunity to learn music from Savitribai. She works diligently for her performance on Guruji's punyatithi (285), as it was going to be her first big performance, "My first chance to prove myself, to show the world what Baiji has given me'" (285). Despite people's retaliation against her performance at the temple, she comes out of it successfully. Hasina appears as a woman with strong determination, who despite her mother's opposition to music, learns it because she was interested in it. Later in her life when she was going to give her first performance, certain obstructions were created on the pretext of her Muslim background. Even then nothing could shatter her enthusiastic spirit and she moves ahead with confidence to give her first live performance. She succeeds in her aim of proving herself as a true disciple of Savitribai Indorekar, a great classical singer.

Through *Small Remedies* Deshpande has projected bold and defiant women who accept the challenges of life boldly and refuse to compromise with them. They make some strong and revolutionary decisions about their lives and strive hard to achieve their aims and ambitions. Deshpande has portrayed women finally asserting their true selves without developing a sense of guilt. Her women represent the image of modern Indian women who want to be looked at as human beings beyond their roles of wife, mother and daughter. The novel exhibits women eschewing their submissiveness and restoring their self-identity by giving up self-denial.

Hence a comprehensive analysis of the later novels of Deshpande—*Roots and Shadows*, *That Long Silence*, *The Binding Vine*, *A Matter of Time* and *Small Remedies*—reveals a gradual change in the personalities of her female protagonists. Women in her early novels are weak and submissive, whereas in her later novels they are more assertive and able to overcome the social conditioning. The female protagonists of the later novels are strong women who have developed selfhood in adolescence but later face identity-crisis in their marital life which they overcome by their power of analysis. These novels exhibit the novelist's mature and developed vision of the quality of life women should possess.

Shashi Deshpande's Feminism: Guidelines for Lacerated Womanhood

The analysis of Shashi Deshpande's fiction in the preceding chapters helps us to understand her feminist concerns, which expound that women should attain selfhood. Shashi Deshpande does not believe in following the established theories and principles of feminism given by the early feminist writers and critics. She believes that the problems of human life can be solved not by adhering to any particular theory but by concentrating on nurturing positive relationships. Her stories and novels talk about human relationships against a purely Indian setting. She states in an interview given to Lakshmi Holmstrom,

> I am different from other Indians who write in English, my background is very firmly here. I was never educated abroad. My novels don't have any westerners, for example. They are just about Indian people and the complexities of our lives. Our inner lives and our outer lives and the reconciliation between them. (248-49)

Shashi Deshpande has revealed the isolated and lonely condition of Indian women whose rights as human beings are axed by the orthodox society. The orthodox society expects the women to be vassals, thus, their self-identity and individuality are always sidelined. Shashi Deshpande's feminism talks about emancipation of women not only legally but socially too. Women are not going to recuperate from their deprived state until and unless they are socially acknowledged as human beings. Even the economically independent women find their lives torn asunder between traditionalism and modernity. Being an Indian, Shashi Deshpande has meticulously and poignantly revealed the Indian social system and the conventional norms designed for its women.

Shashi Deshpande has portrayed the modern, educated, middle-class Indian women who want to attain their self-identity as well as restore their family ties. All her novels depict the female protagonists entangled in different complexities of marital life and relationships they pursue. There is a persistent urge in them to solve the labyrinth of their lives in an effective manner. Shashi Deshpande has portrayed different kinds of women. Her early novels project docile, passive, submissive and weak women like Saru in *The Dark Holds No Terrors*, Sunita, Cynthia, Shantha and Meera in *If I Die Today* whereas Kshama in *Come Up and Be Dead* is diffident; but her later novels project the protagonists who are free from social conditioning. Indu in *Roots and Shadows*, Jaya in *That Long Silence*, Urmila in *The Binding Vine*, Sumi in *A Matter of Time*, and Madhu in *Small Remedies* are the strong women of Shashi Deshpande's fiction who have developed self-hood in adolescence but later face identity-crisis in their marital life which they overcome by their power of analysis. Shashi Deshpande states about her women characters in an interview to Vanamala Viswanatha,

> My characters take their own ways. I've heard people saying we should have strong women characters. But my writing has to do with women as they are. Most of the women I've known are like that—their decisions are made for them. Due to being over-protected, they are people who think one way and do another. (235)

Shashi Deshpande reveals in her novels that modern women are more assertive and confident yet they are unable to liberate themselves from the limitations associated with each role assigned to them.

Shashi Deshpande has projected the trauma of the girl-child in all her novels—Saru's girlhood in *The Dark Holds No Terrors*, Sonu and Mriga in *If I Die Today*, Sonu, Mridula, and Sharmila in *Come Up and Be Dead*, Jaya's girlhood and Rati in *That Long Silence*, Kalpana and Mandira in *The Binding Vine*, Akka's girlhood in *Roots and Shadows*, Kalyani's childhood, Aru and Charu in *A Matter of Time*, Munni and Madhu in *Small Remedies*. Deshpande is the only contemporary novelist in the horizon of contemporary Indian English fiction who has depicted the girlhood of most of her protagonists. Her novels reveal how through her protagonists' childhood, their personalities were shaped and moulded according to the feminine roles they were made to pursue by their families. The Indian society has traditionally insisted on inculcating a particular code of behaviour in the girls. The traits of femininity are considered laudable among the girls, particularly in the middle-class society. The feminine traits of self-abnegation, submissiveness and self-effacement are inculcated in them since they were girls. The novelist has projected the position of girl-children in the contemporary middle-class families and has delineated the social factors responsible for shaping them. She has described the influence of myths, ceremonies and rituals on Indian society and the plight of women due to their sexuality, puberty, child-birth and abortion. She has explicitly and assertively portrayed that girl-children are saddled by their mothers who want to make their daughters their replica. Being themselves a victim of subtle social conditioning, mothers want their daughters to imbibe the same set of values. Mothers are mostly accepted by young girls as the role models. Therefore the mother's responsibility to mould the psyche of a girl is more crucial. Shashi Deshpande states in her interview to me:

> Certainly it matters how girls are brought up. It's mothers who are far more important than the father, because it is the mother who tells you what it is to be a woman. The father is always 'the other.' It is the mother you are going to be one day.

A mother who supports the traditional behavioural patterns for her daughter finds any indication of germinating freedom in her as risky and thus wants to obliterate it. This attitude generates conflict between the mother and the daughter, often leading to a cruel suppression of girls.

Shashi Deshpande has portrayed different facets of mother-daughter relationship. Saru's mother in *The Dark Holds No Terrors* and Kalyani's mother, Manorama in *The Binding Vine* want to saddle their girl-child and are cruel towards their daughters.

Munni and Savitribai Indorekar also present the estranged mother-daughter relationship. The novelist has broken the stereotypical image of mothers, which is always considered as loving and caring. Shashi Deshpande believes that all mother-daughter relationships in the world are not based on love and affection, rather they vary according to their attitudes as a person. In her essay "The Indian Woman Stereotypes, Images and Realities," she writes: "we had to wait for women to write to bring out the truths of this relationship. My novel *The Binding Vine* is to a large extent about mother and daughter; the complexity of their relationship is seen through three mothers and daughters. One of the daughters, Mira, a poet, cries out, 'Why do you insist on my repeating your history when you so despair of your own?' I'm sure this echoes the cry of many a daughter." Simone de Beauvoir writes in *The Second Sex* that the girlchild

> is often concerned in this way with motherly tasks; whether for convenience or because of hostility and sadism, the mother thus rids herself of many of her functions; the girl is in this matter made to fit precociously into the universe of serious affairs; her sense of importance will help her in assuming her femininity. But she is deprived of happy freedom, the carefree aspect of childhood; having become precociously a woman, she learns all too soon the limitations this state imposes upon a human being; she reaches adolescence as an adult, which gives her history a special character. (24)

Suppression of girl-child in childhood casts its shadows on the adulthood of the girls too, making them timid, vulnerable and open to violence after their marriage. *The Dark Holds No Terrors* and *Small Remedies* present this traumatic situation in women's life. The portrayal of the estrangement in mother-daughter relationship in all its dimensions is a unique contribution of Shashi Deshpande to contemporary Indian English fiction. Girls while being saddled by their mothers endure the trauma of social conditioning and gender discrimination—these two factors make them accept their inferiority to men strengthening the secondary status of women in the patriarchal society. These two factors are discussed elaborately in the novels of

Shashi Deshpande and need to be discussed separately.

Shashi Deshpande's novels depict the pain, trauma and humiliation of girl-children due to gender-discrimination that is prevalent in our society. They are not allowed to develop their own identity. Their existence is always side-lined in the presence of boys. Saru in *The Dark Holds No Terrors* recalls that even her birth had been a cruel experience for her mother. She recalls, "But of my birth, my mother had said to me once [. . .] 'It rained heavily the day you were born. It was terrible.' And somehow it seemed to me that it was my birth that was terrible to her not the rains" (169).

Kalpana is labelled as enfant terrible by her mother Shakutai in *The Binding Vine* for transgressing the feminine traits established by the society. Shashi Deshpande has also exposed the Indian society which considers the mothers as complete women only when they provide a male progeny to their families. Often the girls who have no brothers have to bear the brunt of being born girls. Kalyani in *A Matter of Time* has to endure the nonchalant attitude of her mother, Manorama, who could not give birth to a boy. Shashi Deshpande writes, "Manorama wanted a son; instead there was Kalyani [. . .] for Manorama she became a visible symbol of their failure to have a son" (150-51). Even the modern, educated, working women like Vanaa in *The Binding Vine* long to have a son, in spite of having two daughters, "Two is enough. But [. . .] I'd have loved to have had a son" (81). The desire to have a son is equally prominent in men. Mriga in *If I Die Today* has to endure the hatred of her father, Dr. Kulkarni, for being born girl. Manju, the female protagonist, sums up Dr. Kulkarni's attitude as "was he after all, just a traditional Hindu male, longing for a son and an heir? And taking it out on poor Mriga because she was only a girl?" (33). Jaya in *That Long Silence* finds that the family tree has no names of the female members. It depicts that the existence of women in the family is sidelined by men. Thus being in the family, they are not considered as part of the family. In the patriarchal society of India a woman is not judged by her academic records or economic independence but by her marriage and sons. Indu in *Roots and Shadows* concludes about the women of her family, "I knew these women had their own standards for judging people. Nothing about me . . . my academic distinctions, my career, my success, my money . . . none of these would impress. [. . .] To get married, to bear children, to have sons and then grandchildren . . . they were still for them the only success a woman could have" (116). Thus Shashi Deshpande has exposed the bitter picture of Indian society which encourages the women to remain vassals to men and accept their secondary status from their childhood. Vrinda Nabar writes in *Caste as Woman*:

> It is clear that the birth of a daughter is a let down in some absolute sense. A woman who bears a son, on the other hand, is exalted as someone who has fulfilled her mission as a female. She herself is conditioned into experiencing a sense of achievement at having done so. If the other aspects of bearing a daughter (her presence being temporary and therefore an alleged source of grief) enter the picture at all they do so at a later stage. Moreover, they are wilfully regarded as an unalterable situation and in this way the whole boy-girl syndrome is perpetuated and rationalized. (162)

Shashi Deshpande has also portrayed the effect of social conditioning which restricts the total or complete development of the girls' personality as individual human beings. In Indian society, the established religious myths and rituals are highly responsible for proclaiming men as superior to females. The birth of a son is considered a way towards salvation and the carrier of family's lineage. It is the boy who performs all the rites at the death of the parents that gives him a closer link with them than the daughters. Kshama in *Come Up and Be Dead* feels timid when her brother, Pratap, side-lines her existence as a daughter, by carrying out all the rites of their father's funeral. Shashi Deshpande has also exposed the plight of girl-children with the attainment of puberty as several restrictions are imposed on them. The novelist has revealed the psychology of the girl-children who despise their femininity, feel humiliated and unclean during menstruation as they are separated from the rest of their family like a diseased person. Saru in *The Dark Holds No Terrors*, Indu in *Roots and Shadows* and Jaya in *That Long Silence* have to endure the trauma of puberty. Even the biological growth of the girls is made shameful for them. Thus the girls are made to feel themselves physically weak creatures and are advised to possess a sheltering tree, i.e., a man, by getting married. To suit the needs of men, they are taught to inculcate self-abnegation and submissiveness which leads to self-effacement. Shashi Deshpande's protagonists have an ambiguous attitude towards the social pressures in their childhood. They want to overcome it by working and studying hard (like Saru in *The Dark Holds No Terrors* and Indu in *Roots and Shadows*), yet the thought of its complete transgression makes them feel guilty—guilty of deviating from the womanly duties as stated by the society, generating an intense internal conflict (as projected through Indu in *Roots and Shadows*, and Jaya in *That Long Silence*).

Another significant aspect of Shashi Deshpande's novels is the study of the transformation which marriage in the traditional setting brings about in women's life. Due to technological advancement and industrialization in Indian society, the women's outlook towards life and their rights as an individual have changed drastically. The modern women refuse to accept blindly the established conventional norms. Shashi Deshpande has illustrated this new woman in all her novels who find themselves crushed between modernity and traditional trends set by the society. The novelist has delineated that in conventional (arranged) as well as unconventional (love) marriages it is the women who have to acclimatize themselves with the new family and change themselves according to the likes and dislikes of the family, men do not share this onus. By and large, the Indian society believes that success of a marriage depends upon the attitude of women. Jaya in *That Long Silence* is advised by her brother Deenu to become a good wife, "remember Jaya, the happiness of your husband and home depends entirely upon you" (138). Thus, Jaya also tries to become "a smiling, placid and motherly woman" (15-16). Urmila in *The Binding Vine* discovers that Vanaa despite being an economically independent woman submits before Harish, her husband. She states "but her submissiveness, her willingness to go along with him in whatever he wants, makes me angry" (80). Even Indu in *Roots and Shadows* finds herself fidgeting to satisfy her husband in everyway when she states, "Always what he wants, what he would like, what would please him" (54). Saru in *The Dark Holds No Terrors* too submits before the sadistic attitude of her husband. Thus, all the female protagonists of Shashi Deshpande try to acclimatize, adjust and compromise in their marital life. While going through the phase of transition and analysing themselves, according to the roles they are pursuing, they conclude, "It is not that life is cruel but that in the process of our birth we submit to life's cruelty" (92). Thus in their marital life, they suffer due to their submissiveness, servile nature and also due to male chauvinism. Shashi Deshpande as a novelist not only highlights the rigid doctrinal approach of the Indian society towards women but also exposes the women's habit of self-effacement which is the result of social conditioning.

Shashi Deshpande is the only contemporary Indian English writer who has expressed her deep concern regarding the sexual exploitation of women in the society as well as within the family frame. Shashi Deshpande states that it is "a theme which cries loudly to be written about" (2001). Her stories "It Was Dark" and "Intrusion" depict the trauma of forced sex on girls and women. Her works illustrate that the whole social system has relegated women to the status of a puppet where they do not have any right even over their own bodies. After marriage it becomes a possession of their male counterparts. Her stories—"It Was Dark" and "Intrusion" as well as her novels—*The Dark Holds No Terrors*, *The Binding Vine* and *Roots and Shadows* depict the women enduring forced sex within their marital and family lives, reticently. She has also projected that outside the family frame, any kind of sexual exploitation of women is perceived as a stigma on them. Such women are condemned by the society and are not considered as respectable. Shakutai wants to hide the bitter experience of rape committed on her daughter, Kalpana, from the society, as the whole episode will act as an obstacle in consummating her daughter's marriage. Shakutai cries, "'don't tell anyone, I'll never be able to hold up my head again, who'll marry the girl, we're decent people. Doctor,' she turns to him 'don't tell the police'" (58). Shashi Deshpande has also illustrated women being sexually exploited and assaulted by their male counterparts. Saru in *The Dark Holds No Terrors*, Mira and Shakutai in *The Binding Vine*, and Akka in *Roots and Shadows* have to submit to the sensual advances of their husbands. Thus Shashi Deshpande's novels reflect the bestial attitude of men who consider their female counterparts as a possession and not as a companion.

Shashi Deshpande has portrayed the violence and insensitivity of incompatible marriages with a rare insight in her novels. Yet she advocates a healthy participation in life by her women characters. In all her novels she has presented friendship between men and women outside the family framework as a rejuvenating factor. According to Shashi Deshpande, husband-wife relationship is always based on the principle of a master and a subordinate, thus it can never be friendly. A wife can never be her true self in the company of her husband as she keeps on adjusting herself to suit the needs of her husband. On the other hand, male-female friendship outside the bonds of marriage turns each of them into a better human being as it provides them opportunity to be their true selves and ameliorate their personalities. All the female protagonists, Saru in *The Dark Holds No Terrors*, Manju in *If I Die Today*, Indu in *Roots and Shadows*, Urmi in *The Binding Vine* and Jaya in *That Long Silence*, have a male confidant in their lives. Saru is helped by Boozie to realize her true potential as a doctor, Manju in *If I Die Today* and Urmila in *The Binding Vine* have Guru and Bhaskar, respectively, with whom they talk freely about their personal feelings and thoughts, Indu is helped by Naren to understand the disharmony in her marital life, and Jaya is guided by Kamat who helps her to understand her weaknesses as a woman and as a writer. The void of friendship and advice which these women find in their lives due to their husbands' indifference to their desires and thoughts, is filled by their male friends. Thus the friendly relationship of the female protagonists of Shashi Deshpande with men is not a matter of choice or desire for them but a compulsion. Shashi Deshpande claims that such relationship "gives you a freedom to be yourself. I don't necessarily feel that it has to be an affair [. . .]. To me more than anything else it's the cheating aspect of these affairs that troubles me." Shashi Deshpande advocates healthy relationship between men and women which is free from physical intimacy and is based on mental coordination.

Shashi Deshpande has also illustrated in her works the changing attitude of women towards motherhood. She has depicted that motherhood which is considered a boon to women by the society is mostly imposed on them. Most of the time women become mothers without consciously preparing themselves for it or even without their consents. Urmi's mother in *The Binding Vine* fails to manage her daughter as she herself was too young to become a mother. Shakutai also despises her motherhood as she was not financially sound to bring up a child. Mira's motherhood too was also the result of the sadistic attitude of her husband. Shashi Deshpande's novels depict that the women have no resentment towards motherhood but they want to achieve it with a mutual decision. She has also portrayed stray female protagonists who refuse to become breeding animals like the female protagonist of the story "The Death of a Child." Indu in *Roots and Shadows* too decides to postpone motherhood, as she is busy with her career plans. Shashi Deshpande's fiction speaks against the conventional image of motherhood as presented in literature by other writers. Her novels project that the society should look beyond the established frame of ideal motherhood and respond to women as individuals having their own likes and dislikes. Thus Shashi Deshpande has penetrated into the women's world and has revealed realistically the true facet of Indian mothers and motherhood. Her novels depict the women striving to liberate themselves from the feminine traits of self-abnegation and self-effacement associated with motherhood and want their male counterparts to share the responsibilities of parenthood.

Shashi Deshpande has written about the plight of Indian women as she found it in her surroundings. Set against the Indian middle class background, she has based her characters in the present. Shashi Deshpande concedes that the orthodox Indian society is highly influenced by the age old religious faiths, myths, and customs and hence is largely conventional in its outlook. Thus the legal rights are not enough to emancipate women as they cannot save them from social oppression. Her themes reflect that due to cultural and social conditioning, the modern women find themselves leading a life of contradictions which compels them to reassess their lives vis-à-vis the established doctrinations and dogmas. She has revealed the psychology of women who are trying to establish themselves as human beings with purpose in life in a patriarchal society. Shashi Deshpande advises women to develop self-awareness. She states in her interview to me: "Self-awareness right from *The Dark Holds No Terrors*, is important to me, because this is what women have lacked. We have not been told to know ourselves at all. We have been told to accept what has been told to us about ourselves. To me that has been extremely disturbing." Shashi Deshpande finds it difficult to apply the theories of feminist writers or critics especially those who propagate violent feminism, in the lives of women. She states in her article "No Man is an Island" that feminism does not mean "a western concept, rejecting the family and home, hating men and waging a war against them." She further expounds her idea about feminism,

> Today, when I call myself a feminist, I believe that the female of the species has the same rights to be born and survive and to fulfil herself and shape her life according to her needs and the potential that lies within her, as the male has. I believe that women are neither inferior nor subordinate human beings, but one half of the human race. I believe that women (and men as well) should not be straitjacketed into roles that wrap their personalities, but should have options available to them. I believe that nature, when confer-

> ring its gifts on humans, did not differentiate between males and females, except for the single purpose of procreation. I believe that motherhood does not bar everything, but is a bonus, an extra that women are privileged to have.

While going through the novels of Shashi Deshpande, one realizes that the novelist is portraying the plight of the Indian women as evident in the contemporary Indian society and their urge to overcome their suppressed state without negating the family life. Her novels act as guidelines proposing remedies to the problems of women, thus they are panacea to the lacerated womanhood. *The Dark Holds No Terrors* advises the women to overcome the fears which "are inside us all the time" (80), *Roots and Shadows* expounds, that to run away from the family bonds is an act of cowardice since "Detachment . . . was for the dead, not the living" (186). *That Long Silence* suggests that one should have a pessimistic attitude towards life and "Life has always to be made possible" (193). *The Binding Vine* points out that even the worst of circumstances cannot segregate a woman from the family as the protagonist concludes, "Just as the utter futility of living overwhelms me, I am terrified by the thought of dying, of ceasing to be" (203). *A Matter of Time* ends with a note of awakening of deprived femininity and *Small Remedies* suggests that women should face the tragic losses of life boldly and courageously as "dead clamour for release as well" (323).

Deshpande's novels depict the protagonists acknowledging their true self and finally restoring their self-identity. This stage when women come out of their cocoon of silence and assert their true self is true feminism. This is the feministic approach of Shashi Deshpande's works where the women recuperate from the state of suppressed womanhood, and also restore the family bonds. Thus Shashi Deshpande's feministic concerns are constructive rather than destructive. Her works clearly indicate that the concern with feministic issues does not hinder the women's capability to nurture various relationships—of mother, wife, friend, companion and daughter. Rather an awareness of the self as an individual enables them to establish and enjoy these relationships in a more cogent, rational and open manner. She unequivocally asserts that a woman can be a person herself and still enjoy her social roles and relationships fully. Besides this, Shashi Deshpande is a feminist with a difference—she has no revulsion towards men. Rather she points out that men can contribute a lot for the emancipation of women, which is the unique contribution of the novelist in the horizon of contemporary Indian English fiction. The works of Shashi Deshpande have given a new definition of feminism as they do not project the idea that women should compete with men; they rather suggest that the women should develop self-awareness and that the patriarchal society should accept their existence as human beings. The novelist wants the women to recognize and develop their own potential and contribute something to the society they live in. Hence the works of Shashi Deshpande project the women's journey from self-effacement to self-actualisation.

The Fiction of Shashi Deshpande: Women's Journey from Self-Effacement to Self-Actualization (An Interview)

(21 August 2001, Bangalore)

Pall: Your themes and ideas revolve round the dilemma and conflicts of Indian women who are mostly middle class, urban, educated and working. Still you have refused to be branded as a feminist writer. Why?

SD: The fact that a writer writes about women does not necessarily make her a feminist. I am not denying my feminist principles; I have been a feminist and continue to be a feminist, but when I say I am not a feminist writer, I mean that I do not use my novels as a tool to propagate feminism. Any artistic work becomes flawed if you try to use it as propaganda. What you do in a novel is to show life through a certain perspective. Now my perspective is bound to be a feminist perspective. I will be giving you a kind of vision, a point of view which you may not get from somebody else who does not have feminist principles. At the same time I do not say that feminism is good, or that this is feminism. I am pursuing the complexities of human beings. However, much of a feminist one may be, one is really a human being and all those complexities are in us. This is what I mean by saying that I am not a feminist writer.

Pall: But it can be branded as feministic writing?

SD: It cannot be. I would be quite offended, because then you limit my writing. Once you say I am a feminist writer, you are putting some sort of a boundary, an edge around my writing which means that there is nothing else. I deny it very strongly. My writings are not limited in that way. It is about human beings and it is ultimately universal. You know human beings are the same everywhere. Like I said, feminism has given me a certain perspective, a vision which to some extent is bound to come into my novels. Now who would notice that in a family tree the names of women are not there at all. One takes it for granted. But, you know, for me it is important. Now that is the feminist way of thinking. It gives you a vision of how life should be, but it does not mean that life is like that. Life, as I have presented it, is all muddled and all of us have certain different ways of thinking and with so many complexities. So, when you write a novel all these things come into it. It's not one clear line of feminism. No novel can be a good novel if you do it that way.

Pall: Feminism talks of providing women with education and economic independence in order to liberate them from the conventional, oppressive mores of the society. Do you think these two are really related with each other because most of your female protagonists, despite having economic independence, find themselves entangled in the web of female world and also get exploited within marriage, as you have displayed in your novel *The Dark Holds No Terrors*? Do you treat economic independence as a pre-condition of emancipation, as most of your protagonists are economically independent?

SD: Certainly. I consider economics as a very strong motivating force in human life. Ultimately everything boils down to money—that's the bottom-line. But at the same time, it is not enough for women to be educated and economically independent. You understand that society consists of all kinds of people, so even if I liberate myself it is not enough because the world also has to be liberated to allow me freedom to live within it. That is where the problem lies. All my novels are concerned with liberating oneself. It doesn't go beyond that, because that is where I stop, that a person ultimately liberates herself from most constricting factors. Economic independence and education are two parts of it which are very important of course. But there should also be a desire to go beyond what you see and reach the truth. Conventions have given us a certain vision of things, but we have to go beyond to the stark truth, like Jaya in *That Long Silence*, she goes beyond these relationships, husband and wife, mother and daughter, brother and sister and goes to the truth of these relationships. You are free only when you've seen the truths. Education and economic independence are the tools. They can help you, they may not, you may be both educated and economically independent and you may still be bound and wrapped by conventions and brainwashed by the centuries of conditioning. There may be this desire to stifle yourself because you have to live with other people. I have to live with my husband, I have to live with my parents, I have to live with my family. So you keep on cutting bits of yourself to fit into what they expect of you. To me it is more important to liberate yourself but even after that you are still living in a society where everybody is not thinking the way you are. It does not necessarily mean that you are going to be free, but then you are able to at least take the first step, which is for me always the most important step.

Pall: So it is the first step towards emancipation?

SD: First step, absolutely.

Pall: Your concept of feminism suits the Indian environment and social milieu. Your novels propagate the emancipation of women both intellectually and physically while remaining within the family frame and relationships. Thus it is often said that you are not a hard core feminist. How will you differentiate your concept of feminism from other contemporary writers like Shobha De and Anita Desai? Anita Desai has produced neurotic women characters in her novels and Shobha De's women lose their morality in search of self-identity. Marriage to them is a convenience rather than an emotional and psychological attachment as it is in your novels. Do you consider their writings influenced by the western feministic ideology?

SD: I would not rather comment on other people's writing. I mean, there is Shobha De whom I have not read at all. Anita Desai I have read but I would rather not comment because I think it would be very presumptuous of me to speak of other people and what they intend. I am not a student like you who would study their writings. I just read like a casual reader. I can only speak of my writing. Again I repeat that my kind of feminism is what I am writing about and it does not mean either living within the family or living outside the family or living away from it and certainly it does not mean hating men. It means better human relationships and I think this is what has been denied to women so far because you have to live as a subordinate, you have to live as a subject, you have to live as a slave, you have to live as a tool—as a tool to bear children. And none of these are conducive towards good human relationships—not even with other women, because, you know, slaves are not always united by their slavery; on the contrary there is a lot of bad feeling among slaves. So for me better human relationship is what feminism is all about, which definitely includes relationship with men. You can only have better relationship with an equal. For this reason men should also be feminists, because they also have to understand that feminism will give them a better quality of relationship with a woman. A man may imagine that it is nice to have a woman whom he can order about, but he is bound to lose out on companionship. So my idea of feminism is a better quality of all human relationships. To me, the family is important because there is nothing else to replace it. Marriage itself—I am not hundred percent convinced that it is the best arrangement. As a social arrangement, I have my doubts about it. But the family is a very good kind of an institution, because human beings do want to live among other human beings. We cannot survive alone. I think the family is the best we have at the moment. I don't want to give it up. So for me it is very important that any kind of 'ism' which we evolve should not break up a family. I don't agree with this idea that joint family or what you see in these stupid T.V. serials is the best—I mean, everyone staying together. I think these are forced arrangements where things don't work. I would call a family a loosely knit group of people who have many links and ties and are supportive of one another. I think feminism to me is something where women are not all the time suppressing themselves and making themselves less than what they are because they are so afraid of men being antagonised by their competent selves. We are afraid to show our real capabilities because men feel threatened by women. So I think feminism involves men also. I realize that it is very important to include men in feminism. I think that the greatest failure of feminism is that it has not been able to involve men. It has alienated men. They have made men feel that this is a movement which is going to threaten them which is not correct. It is a movement which means better human relationships.

Pall: I think without the support of men it is not possible for women to go beyond the cultural mores.

SD: Men need the support of women and women need the support of men. And we need each other very badly because in this world we are all living together. I would not say that women should be active and men should be supporting. No, I think they are both in it together, equally together only then it will work. So that is my kind of feminism. I do not know which kind of feminism Anita Desai's or Shobha De's is. My feminism certainly does not mean promiscuity. This is not out of any puritan or moral thinking. There are people who are much happier having many relationships. I don't call that feminism. There are some women who want to stick to one man even if he kicks them or beats them. But if a woman has a choice and she prefers to stay with one man—that's her individual choice. Don't call that an 'ism.' So I differ from people who feel that feminism means loose morals, hating men or giving up the family. No it's not at all that way to me.

Pall: Betty Friedan's *Feminine Mystique* insists on treating women as "human." Simone de Beauvoir's *Second Sex* has elaborately and graphically exhibited various stages of a woman's life and the limitations associated with it. These feministic concerns are visible in your works also. You have mentioned in an interview to Vanamala Viswanatha that the writings of Germaine Greer, Simone de Beauvoir etc. "stimulated" you. Have these writers helped you in moulding your feministic thoughts?

SD: Well the funny thing is, like I told Vanamala that time, that I didn't read these books early. I read these writers much late. I had not even heard of the word feminism until a neighbour of mine in Bombay gave me Simone De Beauvoir's book and then somebody else gave me Betty Friedan and then somebody gave me Germaine Greer. By that time my own ideas had become obvious to me. I had some gaps which I filled up from my own personal life and what I saw around me. Some kind of dissatisfaction with how things were and dissatisfaction with the role which I was supposed to play as a woman. For me it was that which really mattered. It was only later that I got the language for my feelings from reading these books, but the ideas were within me. Of all the books, Simone De Beauvoir's book influenced me the most. I don't think that these books influenced my novels because my novels don't come out of books, nor do they come out of theories. They come out of people. But these books did influence me as a person. They coloured my ideas. My ideas about feminism were clear to me, except that I did not even know the word feminism. It took me sometime to realize that there was a movement like that. I was troubled by these ideas, but the climate was totally different in late 60s. I got married in 1964. In late 1960s and very early 70s feminism still had not entered India. I think it would be 1975—the International Year of Women—that for the first time a lot of things were out in the open; so until then these things were not so much talked about, not so much mentioned. Even in magazines like *Femina* you always find stories of girls falling in love, romantic stories. I could never write like that. I could never write romantic stories. It seemed to me so false because I could see the reality behind these things and there is always this disparity. That was the time when feminism was not really much spoken about and certainly in India it was very muted. It was not loud. For me I had to get it through my own life and I felt a confirmation of my ideas through these books. So it was like a confirmation of my own feelings. Though of course the way Simone De Beauvoir put it was mind blowing. To me that book really was something; it opened a whole world to me. I mean, I am very grateful to her. I may not agree with all that she is saying, but she has very meticulously, carefully analysed what being a woman is. And so many of us can identify with what she is saying. I used to see Hindi movies and read books and stories, say of Rabindranath Tagore, wherein you always have women sitting and serving a man. If he eats, he is doing her a favour by eating. If he wants to please her, he will say, "Ma, I am hungry," and I used to think—are these real? When I got my own children I had the same problem again. They tell you so many things about being a mother but is it all real? Am I feeling these things because I have been told about them? I was able to really go beyond what I was told and I think this really was what took me to these writers.

Pall: Social archetypes regarding the status and behaviour of women have seeped into the life of the Indian people and girls are advised to imitate them. This phenomenon is exhibited in almost all your novels. With the growth in industrialization and women seeking independence, how much relevant it is in your opinion to follow these archetypes in the present scenario?

SD: I think any archetype should be looked at very suspiciously. All these mythological stereotypes that we have now and what people keep telling you about Sita, Savitri and Draupadi—how do we know who these women are? They are creations made for a certain purpose. I am not saying that there is nothing real about them. They are very real. Our *Mahabharata* is a wonderfully real book. But the men were the main characters in these myths and the women were kind of props. They filled certain places which were important for women to fill. So if women are expected to behave like that today, it's very false because today's world is an altogether different world. Also we are individual human beings. We have come to this world with some unique qualities. The qualities that I have nobody else has and the quality you have nobody else has. Then why should we try to be somebody else? To me again feminism comes to the same point that I have to explore my full potential. Every human being whether it's a man or a woman, is not just a man or a woman. Men are often suppressed and not allowed to do something because it is unmanly. Mahesh Dattani, a playwright in Bangalore, has written a play about a boy who wants to become a dancer and everybody laughs at him. They look upon it as a womanly activity. Both the sexes have been suppressed. Apart from gender restrictions there are millions of other restrictions. The mythological stereotypes have been used to put women in that place. I think it's very important to recognise that. We may be told that this is how a woman should be—look at Sita—docile, passive, long suffering, enduring. But why should one endure injustice? According to me no human being should endure injustice. Why should one put up with this? These things make life more comfortable for men. To have a Sita who listens to everything makes life very comfortable for you. I can admire certain qualities of Sita but I don't have to admire all her qualities. As an Indian a woman who has been brought up on these myths. I can still read Sita's story and get tears in my eyes, but that does not mean that I want to be like her. I would see Sita's story this way—I have to learn from that. I should not be like that. I will see Draupadi's story and I say I should not be like that. When she wants to marry Arjuna and they tell her to marry all the five she should have said no. Of course it was not possible for her. I recognise that. But today if it is possible for me I should learn to say no. So for me these things are imposed on women. Men are also conditioned by social archetypes—like men are supposed to be certain things—the protectors, the manly, the mature image, they are all part of men. But women are much more conditioned because being in a subordinate position, being the dependent gender, it has been more important for them to follow the path. It is very hard for them to break away since they are economically dependent on man. In a family, woman never had any power. So she just had to be what she was expected to be. For me this whole thing was very important because the day I got married, I realized I cannot play any of those roles expected of me. I can be myself. I cannot be a good daughter-in-law, a devoted wife. I will be a good wife in my own way. I will be a good mother in my own way. So I learnt to shed the role through my own life and I think that is how it happens to many of us. It doesn't come through books.

Pall: What according to you is the major challenge for today's educated Indian women in their family life? In "A Wall is Safer" and "I Want," you have exhibited the feminine characteristic of self-abnegation. In "I Want," the female protagonist accepts the marriage proposal as she has no other choice, whereas in "A Wall is Safer" the protagonist shuns her career for the sake of her husband and moves with him from a metropolitan city to a remote area. However in contrast to this "It was a Nightingale" depicts the protagonist pursuing her career and independence despite her husband's reluctance. What do you think is the ideal way for the educated working women who want to take both the work and family together? What could be a substitute for self-abnegation for women which could help them to assert their individuality and existence without inducing in them a feeling of guilt?

SD: That is a very hard question because I cannot answer for other people. But let me correct you in one thing that in "A Wall is Safer," she is not self-abnegating. She is very conscious and aware of what she is doing. That's what she says: I have done this of my own choice. She has not obliterated herself. She has done it because it is the best choice for her family. And there is a difference between taking a choice, knowing that you are doing it and knowing why you are doing it and going into something passively, feeling that you have no choice and you are pushed into it. That is the kind of thing a lot of women have to do. Women of an earlier generation said that whatever is good for the family is good for us. It's not like that now. Nevertheless women would rather not have a divided family nor would men. If the man is earning more, which is more often true, the choice is simple. The woman gives up her job. But if the woman is earning more, it's going to be a hard choice because I do not know how the man will be able to take it. I keep saying unless men change there can be no real change. In the last 20 years women have changed enormously in this country but the men have not changed at all. That is why our problem has still continued. Women also need to get rid of guilt. To me it is the biggest problem working, middle-class, educated women are facing because whatever you do, you feel guilty. You sit at home without working you are guilty because you are wasting your education, you are not earning money. I was not earning money because I was not qualified to get a job and my son was born within a year of my marriage. So there was no question of my working and I was enormously guilty that I was not earning any money. Today when I look back I am very glad that I didn't go to work because I was able to give my children all my time. But at that time I could not think in that way. I think whatever we do we have a sense of guilt. What is important is to know what we are doing and why. In

"A Wall is Safer," she knows what she is doing. In "It was a Nightingale," the woman is a little stronger. It all depends on your own strength. So it's very hard to give a general answer for everybody as circumstances, personalities and choices are different. I think it's important to know what you are doing and why you are doing it. Whether you want to give importance to your career or your husband's. Most of the time economics decides these things.

Pall: You have portrayed girl child in all your novels. Through Saru in *The Dark Holds No Terrors*, Indu in *Roots and Shadows*, Kalpana in *The Binding Vine* and Madhu in *Small Remedies* you have exhibited the Indian style of upbringing a girl-child. Do you think that social conditioning is responsible for setting limits on women's liberty, as you have exhibited in most of your novels.

SD: Well certainly it does matter how you are brought up. Madhu, for example, is brought up by her father. So there is nobody to tell her that you shouldn't do this. She grows up as a much freer child. Saru is constantly put in her place by her mother. So she grows up with a feeling of resentment and anger as if she has lost something. Certainly it matters how girls are brought up. It's mothers who are far more important than the father, because it is the mother who tells you what it is to be a woman. The father is always 'the other.' It is the mother you are going to be one day. So either you rebel and say I do not want to be like my mother or you take her as a role model. I have seen some very busy career women whose daughters say that they don't want to be like that. They just want to get married. That is one element of rebellion. So I think if you do not have a sympathetic mother it makes you rebel or if you have sympathetic mother, you continue to be what your mother was. Take for example Mira in *The Binding Vine*. She writes of her mother, "Why do you want to repeat your history when you are so despaired of your own?" I think this kind of continued history has to stop somewhere. Some women would go the other way and say that I want my daughter to have all the freedom I didn't have. Others would feel it's safer for their daughters if they put restrictions around them (not because they want to crush their daughters). To me awareness of these things is very important and may be writing can create this awareness. Because when we live our life we don't analyse our circumstances ourselves, we just live. It's only in writing that one stands at a distance and sees it more clearly. I think a reader is also able to see herself more clearly.

Pall: So, do you think that literature can generate revolutions?

SD: It cannot. Definitely cannot. But it can help people sometimes to see their lives more clearly. I don't think literature can change the world. Nor does one write to change the world. I am not writing to change the world or to make the world a better place for women. I am just writing what is in me and what comes out. But if by reading my work somebody gets a better awareness of his or her own life, I think it's a great thing. It is possible that these things do happen but it is not earthshaking.

Pall: Mother-daughter relationship has been drawn in a different perspective in your fiction. A sense of estrangement between the mother and the daughter can be seen in your stories like "Madhu," "Why a Robin?" and "My Beloved Charioteer" and novels like *The Dark Holds No Terrors*, *The Binding Vine* and *Small Remedies*. *The Dark Holds No Terrors* also exposes the deliberate cruelty of mothers inflicted on their girl child. This bold and sensitive illustration of mother-daughter relationship is still new in Indian English fiction and it is also different from the stereotyped image of mother-daughter relationship. Would you like to comment on it?

SD: That's very true. I remember I had gone for a three-day seminar on my work in a Madras college and some girls asked me, "Why are your mothers so unloving?" I thought about it and it struck me that they are neither unloving nor stereotypical. Now no relationship can be completely loving and supportive. It is a myth that mothers are always loving.

Like I said, I had to learn about motherhood through my own experience. I knew that when I became a mother, I was the same person. So you can have angry, hot-headed, gentle, docile, and stupid mothers. It depends on the kind of person you are and your relationship with your child depends upon the kind of persons you and your child are. This is where people go wrong; when they find that their relationship is not stereotypical, they are puzzled. And certainly people expect the mother-daughter relationship to be completely loving. Very little has been written about it in literature. When I was working on a talk about myths and stereotypes, I realised that in our myths and epics there are no stories of mothers-daughters, only of mothers and sons. So traditionally a mother means a mother of a son. Until women started writing, nobody wrote the truth about the mother-daughter relationship. It required the women to write about this. When a man writes about mother-daughter relationship it is entirely different. So this has broken the stereotypes in one way. I remember after reading *The Dark Holds No Terrors*, a professor in a University wrote me a long letter saying that my book reminded her of her own relationship with her mother. And she said that she was so glad that I did not make it come all right in the end and that there was no reconciliation as it would have been very unnatural. "I never had one with my mother," she said, "My mother died unreconciled to me." So these things do happen. I don't call it cruel either. The mother in *The Dark Holds No Terrors* is not very normal. But in *The Binding Vine*, Urmi's mother is a very normal mother. She has her problems, she has her weaknesses, after her husband's death she becomes dependent and it is Urmi, who is looking after her. This is a very normal relationship. And there is always resentment between you and your mother. It expresses itself in little complaints and grievances. These are all very normal relationships. And that does not deny the blood tie. *The Dark Holds No Terrors* presents a very highly abnormal situation. The mother is completely wrapped up in her son and it is the death of her son that completely destroys her equanimity. That's not very normal. That is why Saru suffers so much because of her mother's rejection. Now Savitribai and Munni are another very interesting mother-daughter relationship. And again it's not stereotypical. But again the circumstances are so unusual. So every relationship depends upon the circumstances and on who you are. What kind of a person you are. And I never see that any relationship is the same throughout the world. Every mother and daughter relationship in the world is not the same. There are different kinds of mothers and daughters; depending upon what kind of a person you and your mother are, your relationship takes a particular pattern. I see people as human beings first. And I see them as mothers, wives and daughters, next. We are born as human beings. All these come later. So we try to play these roles, but we don't always succeed because it's not possible for us.

Pall: You have portrayed mothers like Shakutai and Mira in *The Binding Vine* for whom motherhood is not the outcome of a mutual understanding, rather it is imposed on them. But there are also mothers in your fiction who refuse to be the "breeding animals" like the female protagonist in "The Death of a Child." Do you agree with the feminists who assert that the women should have a full control on their womb?

SD: If you are in a marriage and if you have a good relationship with your husband then I think he also has some say in the matter, though I think the woman's right is more important because she is going to bear and deliver the child. But it will be very cruel to say that the man has no say in this matter. Especially if it is the child of two people who have a good understanding and a good relationship then I would say that it would be wrong that the woman has 100% control over her womb. I wouldn't give him control over womb but certainly he should have a say in the decision. But for the women like Shakutai, whose husband is a waster and who really does not want children because it is too difficult to bring up children with no money and no place to live in, such a person I would say can take a unilateral decision. I hate generalizations. I can never generalize; that's why I would make a terrible theorist because theories believe in generalization. I would make a terrible academic because I don't believe in laying down rules. I believe there is no such thing as a general rule. Each human being is different, each relationship is different and the way we work our relations depends upon who we are and the way we live.

Pall: So it should be a mutual decision?

SD: Depending upon the relationship. But certainly not in a bad relationship where woman does not want it, where she is forced to bear a child. Like in *The Binding Vine*, Urmi's friend Vanaa wants a child (a son) and her husband says, "No stop now." So she can't have a child. You cannot call it a cruelty. Though Urmi calls it a cruelty because she knows that Vanaa is not happy with the decision. But one cannot call it a grave wrong.

Pall: "A Day like Any Other" and "The Sweet Antidote" are the stories which exhibit the women accepting their husband's sexual relationship with other women. In these two stories, infidelity is not treated with contempt by the wives. In "The Sweet Antidote," the wife persuades her husband to have physical relationship with the maid in order to ensure a perfect domestic life. Whereas in another of your stories, "The Shadow," the man refuses to accept the illegitimate girl-child born to his wife and in this way never forgives his repenting wife. Do you think two different standards have been set for males and females when we talk of infidelity?

SD: I think "The Sweet Antidote" was a bit of a joke. I wouldn't take it seriously. I sometimes wonder why I wrote it. I was writing a lot then and this was not one of my serious stories. In fact I had almost forgotten it until I saw it in your questionnaire. But "The Shadow" and "A Day like Any Other" are serious writings. "A Day like Any Other" was certainly more serious than that because in it I was pursuing this thought that this woman weighs all that she has against a momentary infidelity. I think it requires a lot of maturity which I gave that woman which I doubt I would now to say that it doesn't matter but I think for woman and man it matters a lot. A man's feelings about infidelity are much stronger for two reasons:

1. In our society a woman is supposed to be more chaste. A man can have affairs and get away with it.
2. For a man his children should be his own. To know that a woman has not been sexually loyal to him implies doubt about his own children.

As Marx said, it has its beginnings in the idea that my property should go to my children. So in these stories men react much more strongly. Above all it is very deeply ingrained belief in all societies, especially in our society, that a woman should be chaste. She should not look at any other man. Even second marriages are banned for women in many communities. They even had Ṡati, so that no man should have access to that woman's body afterwards. These are all dreadful, the extremes of these feelings. Women's objections do not find ways of being expressed. How do you express your objections? Now, of course marriages are breaking up because if a woman has economic independence, she can certainly refuse to stay with a man who has not been faithful to her. But in what other ways can she rebel? Maybe in the bedroom at night, she might refuse to sleep with him—little acts of rebellion which a woman could do. But they didn't mean much. But certainly if a woman infringed the rules she could be severely punished. So I think different moral codes for men and women continue even today. The woman is supposed to be very moral. You have to be so careful about your moral conduct, especially if you are in public life. Men can get away with much more. It's wrong, but there it is!

Pall: Almost all the women in your major novels like *The Dark Holds No Terrors*, *That Long Silence*, *The Binding Vine*,

Roots and Shadows, *If I Die Today*, and stories like "An Antidote to Boredom" have a male friend, a confidant and sometimes a lover. In *That Long Silence*, Jaya goes to meet Kamat in the absence of her husband and Indu in *Roots and Shadows* establishes even sexual relationship with Naren. This relationship enables your women to put their marriage in a perspective and review it. Thinkers like Sartre and Bertrand Russell have supported the idea of extra-marital affairs as it helps people to understand themselves in a better way. Your fiction seems to advocate such relationships. Would you like to offer any comments on that?

SD: I don't think I would specifically call it an extra-marital affair. But I have seen marriages to be kind of restrictive. In a marital relationship—I cannot speak of a man but I can certainly speak of the woman—much of the woman has to remain unexpressed. It is expected of women that certain things are not to be done or not to be said or you have to be a certain kind of person. So the real 'you' remains unexpressed. Whenever I see women talking about their past, when they were children, before marriage, there is a kind of delight in remembering that person because that is the real you and after marriage, motherhood, and wifehood, take away certain aspects of you. It's not that it is deliberately done. It just happens that way, that as a wife you conform to a certain model. As a mother, parts of you remain unexpressed and I also feel the women in India also have a lot of relationships with their own sex, like female friends, cousins, in-laws. You do not have the same access to a male friendship, especially after marriage. I think that sometimes in relationships with the other sex, certain parts of you come alive. A relationship with a male without this burden of sex and marriage seems a very good relationship to me. That is how I think and that is how I have written about these kinds of relationships whether it is Naren in *Roots and Shadows*, Bhaskar in *The Binding Vine*, Kamat in *That Long Silence*. One needs those relationships. Jaya is very much aware that with Mohan she is Mohan's wife but with Kamat she is many things. She is that kid Jaya, a rebellious kid, she is a writer, she is a frustrated person who cannot write what she wants to. She can be angry with Kamat. With Mohan she cannot be angry because he does not like it. So it gives you a freedom to be yourself. I don't necessarily feel that it has to be an affair. Some relationships may move on to that but I think that would make a marriage an uneasy one. To me more than anything else, it's the cheating aspect of these affairs that troubles me. It may not trouble women like Indu. She has sex with Naren and it means nothing to her. Like in "A Day like Any Other," the protagonist thinks that her husband may have had an affair with a girl but in their relationship it means nothing. But not everybody can think that way. I think that kind of a relationship is very rich. Like Urmi has Vanaa in *The Binding Vine* which is a very good relationship but at the same time with Bhaskar there is something more, although the minute she realizes he is interested in her as a woman, she withdraws.

Pall: So you mean to say that women as friend to males are more open and they become themselves?

SD: Yes, with a particular person—it may be a man, it may be a woman. But sometimes with the family, we are not completely ourselves. Like I said, we are continuously restricted by our roles. I am so much the wife and mother here that I may not be able to express myself, my whole self. It's very rare with a marriage partner. If with a marriage partner you are able to do that, it's a wonderful marriage. There is nothing like that, because then there is a freedom of friendship and the intimacy of marriage both combined. But often it is not possible. So it seems to me that a husband cannot be a friend most of the time.

Pall: Besides gender discrimination, you have also presented the plight of women subjected to rape not only in the society but also within the family frame. Your stories "It was Dark," "The Intrusion" and novels *The Dark Holds No Terrors*, *The*

Binding Vine and *Roots and Shadows* depict the trauma of forced sex on women. You are the first novelist to expose the protector as an aggressor in the family. What was the source behind this kind of writing?

SD: I don't know whether I am the first novelist to write on this theme. I would be surprised if I am, because it's a theme which cries loudly to be written about. When I first wrote this story "Intrusion," I never thought I was going to write about rape or about rape in the family. When I wrote "Intrusion," it came to me as a story of a honeymooning couple. That was how it presented itself to me—as the first night of a couple who had not met before. Of course for all Indian men, marriage is a marriage. As soon as you get married you go to bed together but for most girls there is a sense of fear because their bodies have been so private until now. For women sex is not such a strong instinct as it is for men, even biologically or physiologically. So for women, there is a lot of withdrawal, nervousness and fear of exposing their body or letting men have control on their body. But the men never see that and that was how the story came to me that the man is completely unaware of her feelings. I sent it to *Femina* and I rang up the editor, Vimala Patil, a few days later. I was quite nervous and I said, "Are you going to use it?" She said, "Which story—the story about rape?" I was so surprised as I never thought of it as a story of rape at all. Then I realized that of course it is rape. Nobody talked about marital rape in those days. These are all terms which are common now but they were not so common then. These things came to me out of what I saw around me and I never felt inhibitive because rape is for me the grossest violation of trust between two people. Whether it is someone in the family or your husband or any other man who commits a rape, it destroys the trust between men and women. It's also the greatest violence because it is not only a woman's body but it is her mind and feeling of her right to have a control on her body which is gone. So when I wrote "It was Dark," the story of a child being raped, I read a news item in a newspaper one day, about a 14-year-old school girl who was lost and found two or three days later. That was all. I thought, supposing the girl had been raped. What would have happened to her? What about her mother? It is not only the child—but also the parents are equally violated. For the mother it is even more personal feelings because she remembers her own marriage and how she was reluctant to sleep with her husband and how her mother told her not to deny him. 'You have to please him and go along with whatever he says.' That is what a lot of mothers must have told their daughters in those days. For the mother it was like a repetition of this thing in her own marriage. It's worse, more ghastly when it is an unknown person. But a known person is not much better, even if it is the husband. Like Mira, for example, her feelings are so strong about not wanting to sleep with her husband and she wants to say no, but she can't because it is her own husband. To me this is the most ugly and glaring spot in man-woman relationship. It's really very disturbing.

Pall: Husband-wife relationship has been taken as a major theme in most of your stories and all the novels. You have exposed the exploitative trends of the patriarchal society in which man plays the dominating role. The basic instincts of men towards women have not changed. Here I am reminded of Virginia Woolf who believes that progress of both men and women is required to lead a balanced and fulfilled life and also asserts that the potential of women should be developed in a proper direction. Your fiction agrees with the ideology of Virginia Woolf but you also advise your protagonists to believe in themselves and accept the responsibilities of their own life. This offers a new solution and remedy to the fear of losing oneself in the dark labyrinthine passages of the inner and the outer world. Can we conclude that you have expounded a new way for women to survive in this patriarchal society and reshaped the women's ideology towards their life and freedom?

SD: I wish I could agree. It sounds such a big thing. Actually, what I've been doing is exploring my own way towards understanding these things because in each character and story, I learn a little more. It's not that I have all the knowledge. No way. I am just exploring and understanding myself a little bit each time. Certainly I agree with Virginia Woolf that both men and women have to progress because you cannot have men standing outside and women saying that we want this. It doesn't work that way. It should be not a question of what I want. It should be a question of both working together to make a better world. Self-awareness right from *The Dark Holds No Terrors*, is most important to me, because this is what women have lacked. We have not been told to know ourselves at all. We have been told to accept what has been told to us about ourselves. To me that has been extremely disturbing. Long back in 1975, somebody asked me to write about women's position in India. I wrote that 'know thyself' is one of the tenets of Hindu philosophy. But 'know thyself' is only for men and not for women. Women should never know themselves. According to Hindu philosophy or any other philosophy, you only have to know and understand men. You are not important at all. You are just an instrument. To me that was really the most disturbing thing. Even today when people say your novels are open-ended, some people say it's not real feminism because Jaya goes back to her marriage. To me that is not important. To me Jaya knows herself and she can live her life better. Knowledge is so important. It's like opening your eyes which makes you see the world. It's like the sun. You can see the world more clearly. What you do with it, with all that knowledge, is a different matter. But without that knowledge, you cannot do anything with your life. No education and money, nothing can help you to live a better life. I think it's more important to know yourself. To me that's the first step that you have to know yourself, you have to know what you are. Without that knowledge you cannot survive. You cannot live at all. You are not living a full life. You are just surviving. Once you have knowledge, the possibilities are endless.

Pall: The novel *The Dark Holds No Terrors* is an extended form of your story "The Liberated Woman." What made you develop the story in the novel form?

SD: I wrote this story when I was very ill. I was in bed for six months and this idea came to me and I just had to write the story and it was very difficult to sit up in bed but I wrote and rewrote it. I wrote it about 17 to 18 times before I got finally the form which it is now in. Even then I knew it was a bad story. I wrote it for the short story competition of *Femina*. The idea had been nagging me for a long time. Anyway, I wrote it and sent it and got a prize. But I knew it was not a good story. I was quite ashamed of it really. It was very embarrassing for me even to read that story. And I didn't understand why I was so displeased with it. Finally I understood that the whole perspective in which I had presented it was wrong. And then I realized that it's too big a theme for a story. It had to be a novel. To bring all that in the story was very contrived. So I thought I had to write a novel about this. It took me five years to complete it. Before that I wrote *Roots and Shadows* because I didn't know how I was going to write a novel. It was really hard to write that novel. I had this woman, I had her husband and I had this peculiar relationship they had. I began writing and the brother came to me, the mother came to me, the teacher with whom she talks, fortunately he receded and became unimportant, because that was a big flaw in my story somehow. I had written the story through the teacher's point of view because I didn't want to make it a sob story. I thought if I narrate it through the woman's point of view, it would become one of those 'I confess' kind of stories. I didn't want that. So I used the man's point of view to make it a little distanced. But it didn't work. Luckily he vanished from my novel, he had just a small role. It took me nearly five years to complete it. But I knew it was a theme for a novel. I also knew that it was going to be a very tough novel to write. And it was.

Pall: But it's a very good novel?

SD: Well it is a good novel. I don't say that of all my novels. I am very surprised the way I wrote it in one go. Except the end which gave me a lot of trouble, the novel gave me a lot of pleasure.

Pall: Jaya in *That Long Silence* acknowledges her weaknesses and follies as a writer. She accepts that it was her fear of failure as a writer that kept her away from her profession and not the responsibilities towards her family. Do you think that the present Indian women are hesitant in developing their true potential? Has Jaya been portrayed as a representative of average Indian woman who is silent and submissive?

SD: None of my women are representatives of anyone; they are just themselves. I am not writing about representatives. I hate generalizations, symbolism, and representatives. Each woman is individually herself. Jaya is herself. But it is true that for a lot of us fear of failure keeps us away and I think it's very true that for a lot of women your fear of stepping out of your home, creating problems within the family and outside, keep you back. And it's very easy to say that I have no time. A lot of the writing came from my own life because I found time to work. I never waited for time to come to me. I made it possible. I had lots of problems, with children, no money, bad health, and all sorts of problems, but I kept working. It seemed to me that it's always possible to do that, and if you don't do that, you are finding excuses. I don't think that Jaya is a representative but of course there must be Jaya around. I think more than anything else it's a kind of amateurism in women to which I object. Especially among writers I have seen women quite happy to be writing little things and not prepared to take that big leap from being an amateur writer to being a professional. To be a professional, you have to give a lot of yourself. That is where the problem lies, really, because you have to be ruthless. Like Jaya begins by saying you have to be ruthless. You cannot have it all. So you have to give it 100% commitment. Now that is where women really falter. And for that there are a lot of reasons, we are soft, brain-washed, our families come first, genuinely we want to give our children more attention. The solution is not to have children and marriage but that is not possible. For most Indian women, to live alone is a very hard life. So each one of us is trying to find our own way. There can be no generalization. We all are trying to find it in different ways. We all have to make compromises. To me it is important that I would never compromise on my professional excellence that I should give my best. I am not saying that I am an excellent writer, but I would give my best to my writing. I would not compromise, or say I have no time. But the family and children are facts which most of us have to take into account. We cannot say 'I don't care what happens to my family, I am going to write.' It is not possible.

Pall: Your latest novel *Small Remedies* exhibits a mature vision. In the novel the female protagonists like Savitribai Indorekar, Madhu, and Leela lead an independent life and have an independent thinking in the novel. Does it mean that you have given a final shape to the female protagonists of your novels who were relentlessly searching for their lost self-identity?

SD: I don't think so. I certainly hope that there is a mature vision because I certainly hope that I am more mature than what I was ten years ago. Otherwise just getting grey hair and becoming old is such a waste of time! But it gave me a lot of satisfaction because Savitribai has been in my mind for ten years now. It's not that the novel just happened now. More than 10 years I have been wanting to write this novel about Savitribai. What kept me back was that I did not have enough knowledge of music. That kept pushing it back and I wrote *The Binding Vine* and *A Matter of Time* and then Savitribai really came to the foreground and said that you cannot push me aside any more. I had to read a lot. Earlier, I had Indu who doesn't even want to admit that she is doing any writing, there was Jaya who writes rubbish and finds excuses for it, there was Mira who writes but never gets it published. Finally there is Savitribai who gloriously says that my work comes first. Maybe I was moving all the way towards Savitribai. One doesn't know, one doesn't analyse one's work and one should not either, but possibly these were the people who helped me to finally reach Savitribai. I would not say it is a final statement. But here is a woman who is not contemporary. It is interesting that the woman of 50 years ago is the really independent woman. As far as Madhu's independence is concerned, she was brought up differently. She is an orphan and she has to work for her living and is brought up by a doctor, and a different kind of person. All these things made her what she was. Now, Leela is a person who has also been in my mind for a very long time. I lived in Parel for many years. Parel is the hot-bed of trade unionism in Bombay. We stayed in KEM Hospital Quarters. My husband was a doctor there. And just opposite the hospital there is a place called Kamgar Maidan. All the communist party meetings used to be held there. We used to see these meetings going on. Soon after that the Shiv-Sena came and there was a lot of conflict. It was a kind of happening time and all that penetrated into my mind. And then I saw a lot of women who were communist party members at that time. Not from near, I read about some of them—Ahilyabai Rangnekar. I have also seen the kind of social activism which was common at a particular point of time, especially in Maharashtra. There were very socially committed women. So Leela had really entered my mind quite sometime back and I only feel sorry that she was marginalised by Savitribai because to me that again was a very fascinating character and a very true character. There are a lot of women who have lived lives like that. Durgabai Deshmukh was there. Probably Durgabai Deshmukh was in my mind when I wrote about Leela. They all belong to a different era but they are greater achievers than we have today. They all came to me and I am so glad that I wrote about them, especially both Leela and Savitribai.

Pall: In "Rain," "A Man and a Woman" and "The Cruelty Game," you have mentioned and highlighted the issue of the remarriage of widows. Even in contemporary middle-class Indian society, remarriage of widows is not appreciated and promoted. Do you plan to develop a novel on this theme in future as this theme has not as yet been taken by you in any of your novels?

SD: I don't write according to themes. People come to me. I don't take up issues and I don't plan a novel—I am going to write this time about rape, this time about widows. No, that's not the way I write. That would be the dreadful way of writing. For me the people come first. Like Savitribai came to me first. Then I wrote about her. She, as a human being, was more important to me and through her all other characters came. So that is how my novels work. They don't work through issues. It's the people who come to me and the people of course have their lives and their problems. So when I wrote these stories it was not to write about widow remarriage or whatever. I mean if I were to write about these issues I would write non-fiction. I don't think fiction is suited for issues. Certainly not. I can't write that kind of thing. It spoils a novel. I think the aesthetics of a novel sort of rules out anything which is like an issue. By chance I may write a novel in which a woman is a widow and it may be that all kinds of things happen to her. She may marry, she may not marry.

Pall: "The Inner Rooms," "The Last Enemy" and "Hear Me Sanjay" are excerpts from the *Mahabharata*. You have revealed lamenting Kunti and humiliated Amba. A different image of Kunti has been presented by you by removing her mask of endurance. What motivated you to treat these mythical characters as common women and analyze their situation, position, desires and feelings as ordinary beings and not as queens and princesses?

SD: Like I told you I always see people as human beings. I go beyond their roles and certainly I will go beyond their queenly roles. I mean if I can go beyond woman as a mother, woman as a wife and see the human beings behind. Certainly I would see Kunti not just as a mother. I always go beyond the role, behind the role, so it didn't matter to me. But I tell you what really happened was that I was reading Iravati Karve's *Yuganta*. In that she has talked about Bhishma and she has talked about Bhishma's cruelty to women and she said it was unequalled cruelty. So she has spoken of Amba, Ambika and Ambalika and I was thinking of it and I still remember I was sitting somewhere and suddenly Amba came to me and I thought I must write about it. It was not that I planned to write about these people. Amba just came into my mind and I had to write a story about her and I wrote that story. Afterwards I found it intriguing because I wrote about Duryodhana. I went beyond Duryodhana as a king, Duryodhana as a villain, Duryodhana when he is dying and what his thoughts were and I thought that story also came out good. I had been wanting to write Kunti's story for a long time and I had titled it first *Kuntivacha*. Then I wrote a story on Draupadi. People keep saying that Draupadi really caused the war. It is a story with one small episode where Draupadi finds these people conferring and they are going to send Krishna to Hastinapur after Abhimanyu's wedding to talk about peace. She asks: how can you talk about peace and accept five villages? How can you do that when Duryodhana has already said that he would not give you even a needle point of land. They all argue with her and Krishna promises her that they will do what she wants, etc. Afterwards she finds out that all this time, they had been planning for war. It is really how things are in life, because women's wishes don't count. Why should Draupadi's wishes have counted so much that they should have gone to war for her sake? People go for war mainly for economic reasons. They don't go to war for a woman or because somebody pulled a woman's hair. To me it is total nonsense. These women have been given a certain kind of role to occupy in those myths and through the years they have become stereotypes. In the myth themselves, they may not be stereotypes, in fact they are not. Even Shakuntala, in the original *Mahabharata* is not the Shakuntala of Kalidasa. Through the centuries, they have become stereotypes and we have accepted them as they are—that Kunti is a devoted mother, Draupadi is an angry woman, Gandhari blinded herself out of loyalty to her husband. You know, Iravati Karve says that she blinded herself not because she wanted to be a good wife, but because she was angry she was cheated. They brought her all the way from Kandhar, she comes to palace and finds that she has a blind husband. She gets absolutely furious and says, "I am going to punish him." A real devoted wife would have kept her eyes open and would have shown him the world. So I could see so much in Iravati Karve which I wanted to pursue. Iravati Karve was my inspiration, but I also always like to go beyond the roles and I never see human beings as they are presented to us. I like to have my own views. You can't tell me anything, I am going to find out myself. That is how it has always been with my life. So that is how it is in my writing also. I won't take anybody's word for anything.

Pall: Do you think that Hindu mythology has promoted the image of submissive woman in contemporary society? To what extent your sensitivity as an author has been influenced by your early exposure to Hindu mythology?

SD: Certainly Hindu mythology has a lot to answer for. What it has done to women is terrible. Hindu mythology has created through these stereotypes, and now movies are carrying them on. Movies are terrible because this idea we have of Sita and Savitri image really come to us now from the movies and no longer from the myths. How many people read the myths now? So you know it has been kind of taken over and either we have a Sita, a Savitri or we have that angry Devi which is the other side of the image and both are the terrible stereotypes for women to bear the burden. I was not much exposed to mythology as a child because I didn't grow up in a traditional family. But my father was a Sanskrit scholar, people used to come and talk. So it's whatever I picked up from some people's talk. I still remember my father talking one day when I was a child, saying that there are only two heroes in the *Mahabharata*—Bhishma and Abhimanyu—one old man and one boy. I never forgot that and then I read Iravati Karve and when she said Bhishma was a cruel man, it took me some time to accept this because I was so influenced by my father's words. The starting point was really my own pursuit of these things, my own interest, curiosity and desire to know more. Like I said, a desire to think for myself and not accept what was given to me. I was always very invasive in my thinking. It took me a long time to trust myself. Because you think there is something wrong with you when you think differently from others. I did not have the courage or confidence to think that my views were correct. It was the exploration I undertook as a writer which really helped to understand that these are my views and I have every right to express them.

Pall: "The Narayanpur Incident" is quite similar in theme to Raja Rao's *Kanthapura*. Though you have narrated it in the form of a children's story yet thematic similarity is visible in it. Would you like to offer any comments?

SD: Well, I never thought that. Yeah, I know. I am surprised because I never thought of it in that way at all. I hadn't read *Kanthapura*. I read it after I wrote "The Narayanpur Incident." My father wrote a history of the quit India movement in Karnataka and one day he was telling us about it. He was commissioned by a newspaper to write this history. They had asked people who had experiences of the movement to send them in. So my father had a lot of material. I asked him if I could take those papers. He said, "Take it. It's just lying in my loft." So we brought the box home. But I couldn't read the papers because they were all in Kannada. So my husband went through it for me and read out. And then I thought, let me write about this for children. So that was how it happened. It has nothing to do with *Kanthapura*. But I am surprised and pleased too because *Kanthapura* is a beautiful book.

Pall: Among your novels, which do you think is your best and why?

SD: The next one I hope. No, no one can answer this question. It is difficult because each one gives you its own pleasure, each one has its own flaws. I don't read my own work. Once I finish I don't go back. After reading the proofs and all, I am fed up. But I think *The Dark Holds No Terrors* in a way was to me, like I said, more satisfying because one way it was hardest to write, in other way it was more compact—sort of more intense than any other novel. It may be that. But of course *That Long Silence* was really the hardest to write. Because there was really no material there. It is just a woman's thoughts. And that was really in one way extremely hard to write. But I don't know which is the best. I hope the next one.

Pall: By which great writers have you been influenced and inspired? Which is your favourite book?

SD: I don't know which great writers I have been influenced by, because it's difficult to say. But I have read lots of early English writers—Jane Austen is favourite—I don't claim to have any influence of her but I think she is the finest writer ever. Of course I have read Dickens, Trollope, Gaskell, and all the Victorians. The Russian writers—*Anna Karenina* to me is one of the finest books. I have read *Crime and Punishment*. *Crime and Punishment* is another great book. *Crime and Punishment* has left a very lasting impression on me. I've read modern books like *To Kill a Mocking Bird* which I think is one of the finest books. But I think that I would relate to any book with a very strong moral concern.

Pall: The traces of Buddhist philosophy are discernible in the thematic motifs of almost all your novels. In *The Dark Holds*

No Terrors, a couplet from the Dhammapada has been quoted as:

You are your own refuge;
There is no other refuge.
This refuge is hard to achieve.

Have you been consciously influenced by the Buddhist philosophy in your life?

SD: Well, there was a time when I was very deeply affected by Buddha's story, not by the Buddhist thought. For me, it has always been a powerful recurring symbol in my life. The idea of Buddha giving up everything and going in search of knowledge to me has been a kind of very important recurring symbol in my life. I don't claim to be a scholar and I'm not a Buddhist but to me it also has seemed to be a more reasonable philosophy by which to lead one's life rather than the Hindu philosophy which is too metaphysical and which is sort of unreasonable for most human beings, whereas Buddhism seems possible for all human beings. But maybe I was reading the *Dhammapada* at that time when I wrote *The Dark Holds No Terrors*. When I was writing *A Matter of Time*, I was reading *The Upanishads*. So they do appear much more in that. I think that's all. The connection is there. But they are part of me, certainly. I think Buddhism is certainly something which is part of me but so are the *Upanishads* because I do relate a lot to them. There are certain gems of thoughts in it. But I am not a scholar.

Pall: The inner determination of your protagonists, their resilience to transcend barriers or constraints, rational analysis of the cause of their unhappiness and above all their compassionate attitude towards everyone are quite similar to the Buddhist preachings. Sometimes these Buddhist principles are used to present the protagonists' journey towards self-actualization in a figurative manner, as symbolic motifs while at other times we feel that the tenets of Buddhist philosophy form the very basis of your argument. Do you think that the interpretation of your texts through Buddhist philosophy is justified?

SD: You know, once I finish writing a novel it's over for me and anybody is free to do what they want with it. I don't think about it. I don't take too much interest in it. Like if somebody makes a movie of my novel it wouldn't bother me. I wouldn't be excited. For me it's mine until I write it. Once it is published and gone it is not mine. So you are quite free to do what you want with it. It doesn't trouble me. It's quite O.K. Nor am I going to judge whether you are right or wrong. My business is to write. Each reader has his or her interpretation. That is how the connection between the writer and the reader always is. Each reader is going to see something different. I think that's perfectly natural.

Pall: When did you decide to choose writing as a career? What are the comments of your family regarding your works? Whom do you consider as the best judge of your writings within your family?

SD: I never took up writing as a career. Like I said, I just stumbled into it. I wanted to write and I wrote. It became a career because I am a very sincere person, and my commitment is a hundred percent, I mean, I know this is my life's work. Not that I consciously sat down one day and very solemnly told myself that this is my life's work. But it was something to which I gave myself more completely than I had ever done in my life before. I had been never interested in any other thing. I am not talking about my family. I am talking of work. I did my law, I did my B.A., I did this, I did that, and nothing interested me. My father was convinced I would never do anything in my life. But once I took up writing, I myself was surprised the way I gave myself to it, complete commitment. And hard work. I was a very lazy person but worked very hard over my writing. So I just stumbled into it. Found out it is the right thing for me and worked at it. I never called it a career, never had great ambitions, never had great dreams of becoming a great writer one day. Nothing like that. I just wanted to write, I wanted it to be published. I hoped to earn a little money, that's all. At home I am not a writer. My husband is always my first reader, but he doesn't judge. He is thankfully, totally, non-literary. So he just reads it and leaves it and doesn't comment on it at all. I don't know anybody who is the best judge. I think I am the best judge because when there is something bad or wrong I feel it myself. I am quite harsh on myself. It is true that one cannot be a judge of oneself but one can be a critic and I do try to be one. I am a fairly harsh self-critic. So, beyond that I've not given anybody that position. I never had somebody whom I can give my writing to, and get a feed-back. My readers ultimately are the best judge. As a writer, I want people to say my book is good. But that doesn't always happen. Somebody rings me up and says I have written a wonderful book and it makes my day for me. But one day you will get a reaction that it's a horrible book and it will spoil your day. So ultimately one has to become philosophical about it.

Pall: Your novels so realistically display the true facet of the Indian society. How do you select your themes?

SD: I don't select them. They come to me. The people, the characters come to me first. And through the characters, the themes evolve. People come to me as people; since they are people they have their lives and through the complexity of their lives, the themes evolve. Like Jaya and her husband came to me first and I knew they are people who grew up in a pre-independence or rather were born in pre-independence India. That's all. The themes always come out of the people.

Pall: Are you working on any new novel at present?

SD: Yes, I am. I've just started actually. After *Small Remedies*, I was really very tired. I've been working non-stop for nearly 25 years now. And along with work life goes on. So many things have happened in the last, especially in the last 10 years, which have been hard. So I was really very exhausted and I told myself that I am not going to write, but another has come. Only just begun. It's going to take a long time.

Bibliography

Bala, Suman, ed. *Women in the Novels of Shashi Deshpande.* New Delhi: Khosla, 2000.

Beauvoir, Simone De. *The Second Sex*. 1960. Trans. and Ed. H. M. Parshley. London: Four Square Books, 1961.

Collins, Patricia Hill. *Black Feminist Thought: Knowledge, Consciousness and the Politics of Empowerment.* New York: Routledge. 2000.

Deshpande, Shashi. *The Legacy and Other Stories*. Calcutta: Writers Workshop, 1978.

_____. *It Was Dark.* Calcutta: Writers Workshop, 1986.

_____. *The Miracle and Other Stories.* Calcutta: Writers Workshop, 1986.

_____. *It Was the Nightingale.* Calcutta: Writers Workshop, 1986.

_____. *The Intrusion and Other Stories.* New Delhi: Penguin, 1993.

_____. *The Dark Holds No Terrors*: A Novel. New Delhi: Penguin, 1980.

_____. *If I Die Today.* New Delhi: Penguin, 1982.

_____. *Come Up and Be Dead.* New Delhi: Vikas, 1983.

_____. *Roots and Shadows.* New Delhi: Penguin, 1983.

_____. *That Long Silence.* New Delhi: Penguin, 1988.

_____. *The Binding Vine.* New Delhi: Penguin, 1990.

_____. *A Matter of Time.* New Delhi: Penguin, 1996.

_____. *Small Remedies.* New Delhi: Penguin, 2000.

_____. "The Indian Women—Stereotypes, Images and Realities."30 Oct. 1997, Zurich.

_____. "Literature and Morality." *The Hindu.* Feb.2001. 20 March 2001
<http://ch.8m.com//cgi-bin/framed/1179/shashi.htm.

_____. "No Man is an Island." *The Times of India*, 23 April, 1998. 20 March 2001. <http://ch.8m.com/cgi-bin/framed/1179/shashi.htm.

_____. "Denying the Otherness". Interview with Geeta Gangadharan, *The Fiction of Shashi Deshpande*. Ed. R.S. Pathak. 251-55.

_____. "Shashi Deshpande Talks to Lakshmi Holmstrom." Interview with Lakshmi Holmstrom, in R.S. Pathak. 242-50.

_____. "A Woman's World . . . All the Way!" Interview with Vanamala Viswanatha, in R.S. Pathak. 1997. 232-37.

_____. "In Conversation with Shashi Deshpande." Interview with Vanamala Viswanatha, in R.S. Pathak. 256-59.

_____. "In Conversation." Interview with Uma Mahadevandasgupta. *The Hindu.* Literary Review. Sunday. 4 Nov. 2001.

_____. "The Fiction of Shashi Deshpande: Women's Journey from Self-Effacement to Self-Actualization." Interview with Pallavi. 21 Aug. 2001.

Forber, Geraldine. *Women in Modern India.* New York: Cambridge University Press. 1996.

Frieden, Betty. *The Feminine Mystique*. New York: Laurel, 1984.

Gaur, Rashmi and Pallavi. "*The Dark Holds Terrors:* A Story of Mother-Daughter Relationship." *Points of View*, Vol. VI, No. 21, Winter 1999. 73-81.

Haldar, Santwana. Shashi Deshpande's *That Long Silence: A Study*. New Delhi: Prestige.

Hirshmann, Nancy J. *The Subject of Liberty: Toward a Feminist Theory of Freedom.* New Jersey: Princeton University Press. 2003.

Hooks, Bell. *Feminism is for Everybody*. Canada: British Library Cataloguing in Publication Data, 2000.

Jhabvala, Ruth Prawer. *Esmond in India*. Great Britain: Penguin, 1958.

Joshi, P.G. *Shashi Deshpande's Fiction: A Study in Women Empowerment and Postcolonial Discourse*. New Delhi: Prestige, 2005.

Kakar, Sudhir. "Feminine Identity in India". *Women in India Society*. Ed. Rehana Ghadially. 7th ed., New Delhi: Sage, 1996.

Kishwar, Madhu. "Battered". *The Illustrated Weekly of India.* Sept. 24.1989.

Nabar, Vrinda. *Caste as Woman.* New Delhi: Penguin, 1995.

Pathak, R.S. *The Fiction of Shashi Deshpande.* New Delhi: Creative, 1998.

Prabhu, P. H. *Hindu Social Organization.* 3rd ed. Bombay: Popular Prakashan, 1958.

Reddy, Y.S. Sunita. *A Feminist Perspective on the Novels of Shashi Deshpande*. New Delhi: Prestige, 2005.

Russell, Bertrand. *Marriage and Morals.* New York: Bantam, 1968.

Rowbotham, Sheila. *Hidden from History: 300 Years of Women's Oppression and the Fight against It*. Pluto Press: London. 1977.

Sandhu, Sarabjit K. *The Novels of Shashi Deshpande*. New Delhi: Prestige, 2011.

Sebastian, Mrinalini. *The Novels of Shashi Deshpande in Colonial Arguments*. New Delhi: Prestige, 2011.

Singh, Sushila. *Feminism: Theory, Criticism, Analysis*. Delhi: Pencraft International. 1997.

Wollstonecraft, Mary. *A Vindication of the Rights of Woman*. New York: Dover, 1996.

Woolf, Virginia. *A Room of One's Own*. 1984. London: Vintage, 1996.